INDIE AUTHOR CONFIDENTIAL 10

SECRETS NO ONE WILL TELL YOU ABOUT BEING A WRITER

M.L. RONN

CONTENTS

About This Series   v

Introduction   vii

BECOME A WORLD-CLASS CONTENT CREATOR

Lessons in Dialogue   3

Lessons in Comics   6

Lessons from Studying an Interpreter   13

Lessons from Three Assholes in an Airport   16

A Challenging Fantasy Series Idea   19

Audio: The Great Concealer   24

Writing More Short Stories   27

Master Dictation Macro   29

Achieving New Levels of Productivity   37

AI Audiobooks: The Watershed Moment   41

Portfolio Management Achievements   48

Speaking Engagement Success   53

The Idea Well   57

BECOME A TECHNOLOGY AND DATA-DRIVEN WRITER

Lessons in Cover Design This Quarter   63

Building an Easier Master Publishing File   65

Audiobook Proofing with AI Software   67

Fixing a Mistake in a Live Audiobook   69

Bulk File Renaming   71

Clipboard Manager   74

Automating Reviews   76

Lessons in Facebook Ads   78

Another Way to Run Amazon Ads   80
Reevaluating Currency Exchange Rates   82
Selling Entire Bibliographies of My Work   85

LOOKING FORWARD

A Personal Trial   89
Automated Websites   97
The Rise of Cancel Culture   99
R.A.M.P-ing Up My Career   103
Encounter with a Savvy Author Estate   106
This Time Last Year   108
This Time Five Years Ago   111
This Time Ten Years Ago   113
Q3 2022 Progress Report   116

Content Created While Writing This Book   119
Read the Next Volume   121

Meet M.L. Ronn   123
More Books by M.L. Ronn   125

ABOUT THIS SERIES

This isn't your typical writing self-help book. This series is a compilation of lessons learned from an indie author trying to walk the path to success. Follow author M.L. Ronn (Michael La Ronn) as he navigates what it means to master the craft of writing, marketing, and running a profitable publishing business. Learn from his successes and failures, and learn about things that most successful authors only talk about behind the scenes.

To read all the collected volumes of this series in an anthology, visit www.authorlevelup.com/confidential.

INTRODUCTION

2022 continues, and it has been one of the more eventful years in my writing life.

The "time of great forgetting" is in full swing. Summer is the time when writers forget to write. After all, it's nice outside.

Fortunately, the "time of great forgetting" forgot about me. I still maintained record levels of productivity even though the number of books I published this quarter was small. Next quarter will more than make up for it due to the timing of a few projects hitting late in the quarter and my annual Beast Mode challenge, which starts mid-August. This is still shaping up to be a solid year for writing output.

Yet, I dealt with problems. My wife is still battling long COVID and suffered worsening symptoms this quarter. I also had kidney stone surgery at the beginning of the quarter that slowed me down a little due to some complications.

Despite the setbacks, I still made some signature achievements this quarter.

My Core Strategic Priorities

As a refresher, my mission is to create content that entertains and/or educates my audience, preferably both, and to remain nimble in an ever-changing industry. I do this by focusing on three strategic priorities:

- Become a world-class content creator
- Become a technology and data-driven writer
- Become the writer of the future (looking forward)

What's in This Volume

In the World-Class Content Creator section, I discuss experiments with voice recorder dictation that laid the ground-work for doubling my word counts moving forward. I also discuss writing craft lessons learned from bestsellers, collaborating on a book with a friend, and adventures with AI audiobooks.

In the Technology and Data-Driven Writer section, I discuss falling currency exchange rates, running profitable Face-book Ads, and thoughts on new tools that have helped me be more productive.

In the Looking Forward section, I share how my wife's battle with long COVID has impacted my writing as well as thoughts on cancel culture and how to remain balanced in my everyday writing life. I also talk about where I was this time a year, five years, and ten years ago, with a special anniversary taking place this year. It's fun to look back at my career from time to time.

Enjoy this volume.

—*M.L. Ronn*
August 20, 2022
Des Moines, Iowa

BECOME A WORLD-CLASS CONTENT CREATOR

LESSONS IN DIALOGUE

I read a book with a dialogue scene that stuck with me. I decided to study it to see how the author kept me captivated.

I won't share the name of the book because that's not important. What matters is the analysis itself.

This was a 700-word section of a scene between the main character and an ex-girlfriend who happens to be his boss. The main character was just injured in a scary attack, and his boss is visiting him in the hospital, chastising him for being reckless. The scene is a medium-paced (not fast but not slow) conversation between two characters. The scene is mostly witty dialogue.

Here are my takeaways.

1. The author established the setting within the first 200 words. There were three major focus points in the setting. That's an admirable thing to shoot for—amazing setting and world-building early so the reader stays engaged.

2. The author established the secondary character with just three pieces of description, yet she's a

relatively important character in the novel. I've always operated under the theory of *the more important the character, the more details they get throughout the book*. This turns that on its head. It just goes to show you that anything's possible as long as you execute.

3. There is some overwriting in the chapter. There are a few lines that really aren't needed and don't add to the experience. In fact, I don't even remember HEARING these lines when I listened to the audiobook, and I didn't even hear them the second time when I listened to the chapter. It was only when I studied the chapter visually that I noticed them, and even then, my eyes glossed over them. I paid careful attention to the phrases so I can avoid them in my own writing.

4. Approximately 25 percent of the dialogue lines do something other than "said." In other words, the author did something a little different to vary up the conversation every fourth line (on average, not in practice).

5. There were three lines of AMAZING writing in the section I studied (I could argue that there were more, but there were three lines that grabbed me). What if I aimed to write one to three arresting/interesting/very vivid images in every chapter? This isn't necessarily something to aim for; it's just food for thought.

This analysis only took me about 30 minutes. I don't like to spend a lot of time doing this. Studying the craft can become a big time suck with diminishing returns.

I'm a big believer in reviewing a section, carving it up like a turkey extremely quickly, writing down *actionable* takeaways that I can apply in my *next writing session*, then completely forgetting about it. I always keep my takeaways at a very high level and I never write down phrases or words the author uses. The goal when studying should never be to copy, plagiarize, or commit copyright infringement. The goal should be just to see the techniques other pros are using so you too can use those same techniques with your own style and your own words.

I'm grateful to this novel for helping me see yet another way to write dialogue between two characters.

LESSONS IN COMICS

From time to time, I like to change my reading habits. For the last year and a half, I have been alternating between fiction and nonfiction. Specifically, urban fantasy and nonfiction. This strategy has been working, so I don't plan to fix it.

But every once in a while, I like to read something out of left field. I don't remember how or why I stumbled upon comics, but I made a split-second whim decision to read IDW's *Teenage Mutant Ninja Turtles* comics. This series is a fresh retelling of the *Teenage Mutant Ninja Turtles* story that began in 2011 and, at the time of this writing in 2022, is still going strong.

I have never confessed it publicly, but I have always been a big TMNT fan. I grew up with the 1987 series, and I played the Super Nintendo games *Turtles in Time* and *Teenage Mutant Ninja Turtles: Tournament Fighters* games to death during my childhood. And, of course, I watched the live-action 90s films many times. I have many fond memories of my childhood time with the Turtles.

I also enjoyed the 2003 animated series, which I thought was a lot darker and more mature compared to the 1987 series.

I know my Turtles terminology and characters (in their various iterations) down cold.

I wasn't sure what to expect when I started reading the IDW series. Many people raved about it. At first, I wasn't so sure. I have always thought that the Turtles' origin story has always been a bit hokey. There's just no good way to get from real turtles to mutant turtles without a few mental gymnastics and suspension of disbelief. The IDW comic definitely is the best origin story for the series.

There is so much that the series does right, and I binge-read the entire thing because it was the most fun I had reading this year. Without getting into the characters or story too much, there is so much I took away from this comic series that inspired me to write better fiction.

Teams

The *Teenage Mutant Ninja Turtles* is one of the most iconic teams in entertainment. When most people think of teams, they think of teams with humans, like the *A-Team*, *Star Trek*, *Grey's Anatomy*, and many others. Most people don't put the *Teenage Mutant Ninja Turtles* in the same sentence as a team, but teamwork and brotherhood is the central theme of the series.

The Turtles are four brothers who must stick together no matter what. Leonardo is the leader of the group and the most disciplined, who serves as an elder brother. Raphael is a hothead and a defender, practicing vigilante justice in his free time. Donatello is the brains of the operations. Michelangelo is the immature youngest brother who just wants to have a good time no matter what he does. Combine these four brothers with

Master Splinter, a quiet but profound father who serves as their mentor and martial arts sensei, and you have one of the most legendary teams ever made.

The IDW comic amplifies the team aspect of the franchise. It does things with teams that I have never seen before.

The Turtles and Master Splinter are the core team, but other good guys float in and out depending on what is going on in the story. There is April O'Neil, the human who discovers the Turtles and befriends them. There's also Casey Jones, April's love interest, and a fellow vigilante along with Raphael. And there are many more. The "good guy" team is quite large and varied. Generally, each issue arc of the comic (about four issues) focuses on two to three good guys at a time. The others take the backstage.

There is also the Mutanimals, led by Old Hob, who is a mutant cat who was exposed to Mutagen at the same time as the Turtles. Old Hob starts off as a villain, but alternates between good and evil depending on what his goals are at the moment. He has a team of other mutants around him.

But there's a bad guy team too. There is Shredder, who needs no introduction. Shredder has a second-in-command, who is his granddaughter Karai. There's Baxter Stockman, an evil scientist who works for whoever is most expedient at the time. There are Bebop and Rocksteady, two mutant goons who do Shredder's dirty work. There's Hun, a former gang boss off the street who also does Shredder's dirty work (and is Casey Jones's father). And then, of course, there is the entire Foot Clan of ninjas that work for Shredder. Shredder works with Kitsune, a god who helps him see visions of the future and cast spells.

And then there are the really bad guys, led by Krang, an evil alien from Dimension X who is trying to restore his dying race of aliens to former glory. Krang has minions that serve him too.

So, really, this comic is a battle between four different teams. One good, one sometimes good, one bad, and one really bad. It's a masterful lesson on how to interlock teams and their different storylines together.

This comic taught me that when executing a team, it is best to think about two components:

- Who's on stage
- Who's in the spotlight

Who's on stage is who is in the scene. For example, the four Turtles might be doing a night run on the rooftops.

Who's in the spotlight is who is driving the scene. For example, the Turtles might be arguing about Donatello's plans to destroy the Technodrome, so Donnie is in the spotlight and he gets the most lines and the most face time.

In any four-issue arc, two to three good guys will be in the spotlight as well as two to three bad guys. Then, that arc ends. The next arc picks up where the previous one left off, but this time through the lens of another character.

Micro Series

Another great feature of this comic is the micro series. In the first few volumes, there is an issue devoted to one of the team members from each team.

Leonardo's issue is about him focusing on his training and inadvertently catching Shredder's attention, something that will haunt him later.

Raphael's is about vigilante justice.

Donatello's is about Donnie sneaking away to a scientist conference and meeting a man who becomes his rival and friend.

Michelangelo's is about Mikey sneaking off to a costume party, discovering a heist in action, and apprehending the bad guys.

And so on. The micro series are wonderful character studies. In many cases, what happens in the micro series has a direct impact on the plot later in the bigger arc, and the reader is so much more invested as a result.

I was also blown away by how this was executed. One lesson I have learned in my fiction lately is just how problematic origin stories can be. In comics, origin stories are expected; they are one of the main comic book tropes. But in fiction, origin stories can't be executed in the same way. If book one of a series is an origin story, readers will go into the sequels with expectations that the sequels will be similar to the origin story. But structurally, that is not possible.

In any origin story, there is the hero before the transformation, the events leading up to the transformation, the transformation itself, and then the hero learning how to adjust to their powers.

In a sequel, the character already has their powers and is somewhat comfortable with them. Books two and onward will be more similar to each other than to book one. If you take a few books to hit your stride as an author, you aren't giving your series the best possible chance. This is why origin stories can be problematic with fiction. It's also why many best-selling indie authors start their series with their characters already comfortable with their powers, and these authors reserve origin stories as prequels and/or list magnets. I never truly understood this until recently.

There's also something to be said about having a repeatable

structure in every book. It makes the reader comfortable. They always know what to expect whether they are buying book one or book nineteen. There is power in that.

Anyway, back to the micro series. I would like to try to do something similar with my next fiction series using the lessons I learned from reading the micro series. It might take the form of a short story collection that collects the characters' origin stories. Or, I might find a way to weave a micro series into the main narrative. I'm not sure yet, but it's got me thinking.

Annuals

If you have ever read a comic series, then you are no doubt familiar with annuals. In an annual, which is usually the last issue in a collected volume, the art style, storyteller, and the overall aesthetic are different. The story, while often continuing the narrative in some way (but not always), is told by a different team of artists and writers. Annuals give great opportunities to new voices to showcase their skills.

To apply this to my fiction, I don't plan on inviting anyone to write in my worlds, though that is certainly one way to do it. Instead, it would be fun to take an annual approach to the main narrative in some way. For example, maybe I do certain things in every novel at a predictable point that changes up the narrative while still continuing the story. Or, this could be a short story collection or series of novellas. Again, at the risk of repeating myself, I'm not sure how this will manifest itself in my fiction just yet, but it left an impression on me. I normally don't like annuals that much because in previous comics I have read, they never grabbed me. IDW's *Teenage Mutant Ninja Turtles* annuals are one of the few that I have enjoyed in all the comics I have read, and I do like comics.

I am looking forward to how these inspirations will one day show up in my fiction. I learned a lot from this comic series, and I am sure that it will be one that I read again in the future.

LESSONS FROM STUDYING AN INTERPRETER

I had to attend an insurance training for my job. The training was at a hotel business conference center, and it was a nice way to get out of the house for a few days.

I have attended these types of training many times, but this time was the first time one of the participants was hard of hearing and needed the assistance of an American Sign Language (ASL) interpreter.

The interpreter sat in a chair in the front of the room. For eight hours, she translated every single thing that was said in the room, even questions from other participants.

I cannot stress enough how difficult a skillset this is. It's one thing to listen to someone, pause, and interpret what they say. It's another thing entirely to interpret what they're saying in real-time. I still can't truly wrap my head around how one could do this. I suppose your brain has to be wired a certain way.

Studying the interpreter was a great people-watching session. For starters, she wore all black. I've seen interpreters do this so that the participants have an easier time focusing on their face and hands. I have seen other interpreters who didn't wear black, though, so this doesn't appear to be a requirement for the profession.

She kept one eye on the instructor at all times, alternating between facing him and the participant who needed her assistance.

She was extremely expressive in how she moved her hands and face, almost as if she were talking to a child.

Some words just can't be translated into sign language in any meaningful way. These terms include "commercial general liability", "asbestos", "nano materials", and many more torturous insurance terms that were uttered repeatedly throughout the training. I felt bad for her until I realized that she would just mouth the term to the participant rather than sign it.

During a break, the interpreter admitted to everyone that she had never read an insurance policy let alone attended an industry seminar. A few people's heads exploded.

During breaks, she spoke almost exclusively to the participant she was working with. She continued to sign and have conversations with him even when she wasn't actively interpreting. I could tell they shared a special connection even though they had never met each other.

Throughout the training, the other participants were just as captivated and intrigued by the interpreter as I was. I would frequently catch the other participants glancing over at the interpreter right after the instructor said a difficult word, just to see how she would interpret it. During breaks, there were many sidebar conversations about how great the first interpreter was.

On the second day, the wonderful interpreter was replaced by another whose skills were just as adept, but she did not have the same connection with the participant. In fact, I rarely saw her speak to him during breaks. She did not socialize or mingle with the other participants, and when it was time to go home, she was the first one out of the room.

In conclusion, I was glad for this people-watching experience. It taught me a lot about the interpreting profession and how I might write an interpreter into a story one day. It also illuminated more facets of that ever-morphing and infinite diamond that is human nature.

LESSONS FROM THREE ASSHOLES IN AN AIRPORT

While traveling home from a writing conference, I got stranded at O'Hare Airport in Chicago. O'Hare is one of my least favorite airports, but I won't get into that. I found myself staring at a delayed flight with an extra three hours to kill.

I had planned on being home in the early afternoon, but now I wasn't going to be home until after dinner. As a result, I was going to be at a serious deficit in my daily word count.

I needed to get words in. I was working on *Year of the Rat* (The Chicago Rat Shifter Book 3) and I was close to finishing it, so I didn't want to waste any time.

I'd brought my voice recorder with me, but I forgot my lapel microphone, so I had to hold the recorder directly to my mouth. This wasn't ideal, but lately, I have been disciplined when it comes to my daily word count. I don't care how I get the words as long as I get them and they are as close to first-draft final as possible.

The concourse I was stuck in had a hallway that served as a loading area and supply transport for the United and Delta airport lounges. The hallway was long, quiet, and had almost no foot traffic. I found a secluded corner and went to work with my dictation.

Several chapters later, three African American men passed by. They made remarks about me that I won't repeat. They didn't say them to me directly, but they made sure that I heard them. They laughed at me and then kept going. The experience left me feeling insulted and upset.

Now, I will be the very first to admit that I put myself in that situation. After all, I was sitting in a dark hallway, speaking into a voice recorder like a crazy person. I suppose I deserved to be laughed at, or at least stared at with a little curiosity. But what they *said* was what bothered me. It was uncalled for.

I took a walk, listened to some music, and forgot the encounter until it was time to write this chapter.

The experience got me thinking about those guys and what kind of people would make a comment like that. They represent a type of person I haven't written about in fiction before.

There are some in the black community who believe that black people must behave a certain way, particularly males: you've got to be hard, have street cred and swagger, and fall into the typical black stereotypes. If you don't fit that mold even a little, you're worthy of contempt because you're not black or manly enough.

I feel sorry for these people because they've usually suffered some sort of trauma in their lives and are subconsciously offloading it to others. In other words, they're manifesting their hurt by trying to hurt other people.

As I walked through the airport reflecting on my emotions after the encounter, I decided to turn that negativity into something positive. Writing this chapter was one way to neutralize that negative energy.

Growing up, I was bullied by a fair share of black men like

this. These bullies treated me badly, but it was only because they were jealous.

My encounter with those three men took me back to my middle school and high school days when I endured treatment like that daily. I was frequently called an "Oreo" (black on the outside, white on the inside). I got into a lot of fights.

My childhood experience is one reason why I prefer to spend most of my time alone, and why I am extremely selective about who I surround myself with. I have no patience for negative people.

Most of those people who bullied me in my childhood have done nothing with their lives; in the end, I became successful in spite of them.

What's the difference now between me yesterday and me today?

First, I've gotten a lot older and had time to reflect on my life. I'm not bitter about things like I used to be when I was young. When I was younger, an experience like the one in the airport would have made me upset and moody for weeks. Today, it bothered me for a few minutes and then I quickly forgot about it because my novel was much more important than the opinions of some random strangers that I will never see again.

Second, I'm a writer. The three men in the airport represent a character that I've never written about in my fiction yet. At some point, I'll write a character based on these guys because I think there's strong material there.

Black folks complain about racism in the United States, and while it's true that there is racism in this country, no one treats us as badly as we do ourselves. Not by a long shot. That's worth exploring in a novel someday.

A CHALLENGING FANTASY
SERIES IDEA

I came up with an idea for a new series this quarter. It will be my most challenging series yet, but I'm excited about it.

However, it's going to require a lot of research. It's also a very tricky concept from a marketing perspective—maybe one of the trickiest I've ever come up with.

The initial concept is a mythological urban fantasy story, with a flavor of superheroes. This just so happens to be a pretty hot genre right now. I didn't plan it that way. The idea just happened.

I've seen people fight to the death on whether superhero fiction can be considered urban fantasy, or vice versa. I generally think that superhero fiction and urban fantasy are mutually exclusive, but there is a lot of overlap. The trick, if I were going to do it, is to adhere very, very carefully to all the main tropes in every overlapping genre that the concept touches:

- Fantasy: there is a conflict between good and evil and the good guys win, there is a team of good guys, there is magic, and there is a magic system.

- Urban fantasy: takes place in a real city, there is magic and it is hidden, and there are supernatural creatures.
- Mythology: the characters from the mythology feature prominently in the story, the heroes are linked in some way to those characters (or are gods themselves), and the mythology serves as the tapestry and impetus for the story.
- Historical: any historical sections need to be accurate and believable. They don't need to be 100 percent historian-approved, but I do need to do my best.
- Superhero: has to play by the rules of UF, but also have origin stories, a strong team, supervillains with a strong team around them and a good rogues gallery, no crazy multiverses (this isn't typically done in UF). There should be no science, aliens, or space travel (those don't play well with the fantasy genres listed earlier).
- And so on.

Holy crap. This is a huge challenge for someone who writes into the dark. And I haven't even gotten started on what the book cover or book description should look like.

If I do this series, I'm going to follow some important steps based on key lessons I've learned over the past few years since making urban fantasy my main genre. These will hopefully set me up for success:

1. I'm going to write the entire series, or at least the first three to five books, before talking about the actual concept. I may honestly do five books, which is a little crazy, but this concept is so challenging

that if it doesn't work, I would prefer to have it fully formed and stand on its own as a complete set so I can move on if I want to.

2. Regardless of what the market says, I'll still finish the idea. I don't abandon ideas once I commit to them. You never know how reader tastes will change.

3. I'm going to structure the series so that it can go on for a very long time, at least for 20 books. I keep saying I'm going to do that, and I did it with *The Good Necromancer* finally. This time, I'm going to do it better.

4. I've really got to do my research on some of the historical and mythological elements in the story. This will definitely be the most challenging research I will have ever done, and the stakes are pretty high if I screw up. Fact-checkers will be doubly important with this series. The concept is 50 percent material that I know well and 50 percent material that I don't.

5. I am going to design the covers backward. That worked like magic with *The Good Necromancer* series. So, if I write five books, I'll start by designing Book 5 first, then work backward. Once done, I will pick the strongest one and make *that* the Book 1 cover.

6. I may not put a stock model on these covers. You can find as many white people as you want to put on book covers; black people, not so easy. I'm honestly tired of fighting this battle. Illustration is an option, but it may be a bad choice 1) because it's expensive 2) because of the genre-targeting I mentioned above and 3) because just because you illustrate it doesn't

mean you'll nail it. Illustrating a series with 20+ book potential is a ridiculously expensive mistake if I get it wrong. According to K-Lytics (a data and analytics company that specializes in self-published data on Amazon), over 90 percent of urban fantasy titles have people on the cover. Over 60 percent of those are females. Around 30 percent are males. Only 10 percent of books in the genre have symbols on them. This story has a male character, which already puts it in the minority. If I go with symbols on the cover, I am already potentially operating with two gigantic strikes against me unless I found a way to NAIL the concept without a person, which I think can be done, but carefully. Symbol-driven covers are usually the province of epic and high fantasy (and thrillers and mystery too), but I think I could get away with it by 1) being smart about the background, using it simultaneously to convey urban fantasy AND mythology and 2) strong and bold typography. Symbol-driven covers have downsides, but they have the advantage of being cheaper and easier to sustain long term. It's much easier to hire someone to illustrate a symbol than it is to illustrate a person. Also, it's much easier to do these types of covers yourself if a designer builds you a strong template. Again, these are little talked-about reasons to consider symbol covers. I'm still early in my thinking, so this could change.

7. I'm going to run a Kickstarter campaign to test the idea. If the Kickstarter fails, the series will probably fail. I will, of course, have all the novels done, edited, and packaged before running the Kickstarter.

8. This story is going to have a strong team. There will be a central main character, but I'm going to use a bigger team instead of the two to three characters that I usually do. The villain will also have a team. I do this in my novels already, but I'm going to be a bit more intentional about it.

9. There will also be some romance, though it won't be substantial.

10. I am going to avoid the thing I screwed up with my last two series without realizing it until it was too late. Books 1 of *The Good Necromancer* and *The Chicago Rat Shifter* are origin stories. That resulted in Book 1 being different structurally from the sequels in the series. For example, with *The Good Necromancer*, I follow a very specific structure with Books 2 and onward that doesn't exist in Book 1. My theory is that there is probably some cognitive dissonance there. That said, the series has a very good read through and I wouldn't change a thing about it. I think it would have been better if I had executed Book 1 differently, though.

Anyway, that's a lot of information about a concept that's early in my head and still evolving every day. But I'm excited about it, and regardless of how it shakes out, I will have a lot of fun writing it. I look forward to cataloging my experience writing it in future volumes of this series.

AUDIO: THE GREAT CONCEALER

I was listening to a fiction audiobook that I enjoyed immensely. In fact, I enjoyed it so much that I listened to it twice.

The novel taught me a lot about characterization and dialogue. As with all novels I read that I enjoy, I study them afterward to determine how the author kept me spellbound.

When I loaded the e-book edition and reread the chapters I loved, I noticed something strange. The pages didn't *look* like what I was used to.

When I read the works of a mega-bestsellers, I am used to seeing shorter paragraphs and sentences for faster-paced scenes, and the opposite for longer-paced scenes. Most scenes fall somewhere in the middle.

This novel didn't follow that rule at all. The fast-paced scenes were big and blocky, and the slow-paced scenes were even bigger and blockier. This broke some of the rules that I know mega-bestsellers adhere to.

The author that wrote this book was *not* a mega-bestseller (though they are extremely successful in their own right, and, in my opinion, one of the best practitioners in their genre).

I thought about this disconnect a lot, and I came to the

following conclusion: audio is a very good concealer. It masks issues that would otherwise turn off e-book and print readers.

Here's why:

Audiobook listeners usually consume audio while they are multitasking. I myself listen to audiobooks while doing the dishes, driving, and mowing the lawn.

When people are listening to audiobooks, they simply don't use the time-scrubbing feature most of the time. Audiobook apps allow you to skip ahead and jump back in intervals, such as 30 seconds. If you're driving to work and listening to an audio-book, you aren't going to use those buttons. If you're doing the dishes, you aren't going to touch the screen with wet hands unless you really need to. In other words, you have no choice but to listen to whatever happens.

Many audiobook listeners consume audio at higher speeds, such as 1.5x or 2.x, so they don't hear issues with craft as readily.

Narrators will often intrinsically correct pacing issues through their narration. They will narrate fast-paced scenes faster and with more animation, for example.

Some people listen to books almost exclusively in audio. They may never see the e-book or paperback editions.

When you consider these facts, you can get away with a lot of bad habits, such as improper pacing and overwriting.

Remember, the listener isn't going to skip past it and isn't going to think too much about whether the book is overwritten unless the author goes over the top.

Ironically, this novel was extremely long. I would argue that it was twice as long as other books in the genre and filled with approximately 15 to 25 percent filler descriptions. I'm not knocking the book because I still enjoyed it, but I can't deny what I saw.

My point is that you can get a lot of mileage out of an audiobook. If you're still improving your craft, audio will hide many of your flaws. As long as you write a story that is *good enough*, readers will buy the audiobook, and they will enjoy it.

If you pad your story with filler, maybe spend more time and money promoting the audiobook version—readers won't know the difference. I don't plan to use this tip for evil; I'm just telling it like it is.

WRITING MORE SHORT STORIES

I love writing short stories. There was a time in my writing career when I wrote them exclusively. I once told a friend that I couldn't imagine writing a novel because they were so intricate and complex.

Now, at this stage in my career, I almost exclusively write novels.

Once I published my first novel, I stopped writing short stories. When you step onto the novel train, it demands all of your time, energy, and attention. Suddenly, the only thing you care about is writing more novels. More novels mean more stories to get lost in, more readers, and more money. It's an intoxicating drug.

Yet, novels take much longer to write than short stories, and they come with higher risks.

I've been saying for a while that I want to write more short stories, but I haven't put my words where my mouth is. This year, I committed to taking small steps to change this over the medium term.

First, I started reading more short stories this year.

Second, I wrote two short stories in my *Good Necromancer*

series. Both stories were approximately 5,000 words, and I followed the Lester Dent plot formula. I had a great time writing the stories. I licensed one story to an upcoming urban fantasy anthology; I have been shopping the other story around to fantasy magazines. That was a meaningful step.

Third, I responded to a push from a mentor. The mentor asked me what my strategy was for short stories, and I gave him a squishy response--something about wanting to grow my short story portfolio over time. He asked how many unpublished short stories I had. The answer was about 12. He challenged me to submit one of those unpublished stories to a magazine market within the week. His advice was that magazine submissions take a long time, so it's best to ease into the submission process so that you start getting answers (acceptances or rejections) in a steady stream. But it takes a long time to build up to that steady stream.

I listened and submitted three short stories to different markets this quarter. It's not much, but it's a start.

My thought is that if I can write and submit one short story per month, that will eventually get me to the goal state that my mentor recommended. I'm not there yet, and it's going to take me a while to build short stories into my workflow, but I'm excited about it.

The hardest problem I have right now with short stories is getting back into the short story mindset. Since I have developed a novel mentality, it has been difficult for me to transition back to simpler short story structures. I like the short stories I wrote this year, but I still think they have a novel mentality. It's going to take me a while to disabuse myself of that.

I look forward to talking about more short story endeavors in the future.

MASTER DICTATION MACRO

In the previous volume of this series, I discussed my adventures with a voice recorder dictation—an advanced but superpowered way of writing stories with insanely high daily word counts.

I'll recap my process here:

1. I use a Sony UX 570 voice recorder that I purchased on Amazon for approximately $70. Voice recorders are engineered to capture the human voice, and they do a much better job of it than smartphones.

2. I purchased a harmonica neck holder and put the voice recorder inside the holder. I put the holder around my neck and dictate while walking around and multitasking. This ensures that the voice recorder is approximately two inches away from my mouth at all times. No matter what I'm doing or how I am moving, this ensures more accurate dictation and transcription.

3. When I'm in public, I use a lapel mic hooked up to my voice recorder so people don't think I'm *completely* crazy.
4. I also have learned to enunciate more and speak more exaggeratedly when I am dictating. This also ensures more accurate transcription.
5. I upload my audio to Dragon and use its transcription feature. Transcription takes approximately 10 to 20 percent of the time it takes to dictate.
6. I put my transcribed audio into Microsoft Word.

And that, my friends, has been an unbelievable boon to my word counts. However, this method comes with problems:

1. You still have to speak in "Dragonese," meaning you have to speak with dictation commands. (Another option is to hire a transcriptionist, but ain't nobody got the money for that.)
2. The cleanup is absolutely, positively horrendous. Anyone who has dictated stupendous word counts and then had the unfortunate displeasure of editing those words can tell you that this is extremely painful.

I have spoken with several authors who use voice recorder dictation. For them, the speed at which they can fly through their stories outweighs the disadvantages of the cleanup (which they admit is painful).

But...you should know me well enough by now to know that dictating crazy word counts and spending hours cleaning them up is not my cup of tea. At all.

I tried to solve this problem using... wait for it... technology and automation!

I have spoken at great length about Microsoft Word macros in previous volumes, so I won't explain them here other than to say that they are the best way to solve this problem that I can think of.

I came up with a two-part idea. The first part was to create dictation commands that I used while speaking that would allow me to edit and format my text in real-time as I was dictating. The second part of the idea was to create a Microsoft Word macro that identifies those dictation commands in the transcribed text and takes certain formatting actions based on the commands. The macro then deletes the commands afterward so it looks like they were never there. The macro would then make edits in the document as tracked changes. I could then review and accept all of the changes with the click of a button.

This macro is *the* signature accomplishment in my writing business this year.

Here is a recap of the commands and the macro.

COMMAND #1: Delete the current sentence. When you're dictating, it's not uncommon for your mouth to move faster than your brain. You might say a sentence, but realize that you said something incorrectly. Or, you may have used a word you didn't mean to use. Whenever this happens, I say the command "Pikachu period." The macro will then delete every sentence that contains that phrase. This is wonderful editing in real-time. When I make a mistake, I can simply say the phrase quickly and then say what I meant to say. You would not believe how much time this saves.

(You're probably wondering...why "Pikachu"? Because it's an easy word to say and there are no words in the English language that sound quite like it. If you teach it to Dragon, it will recognize it correctly most of the time. Plus, it's fun to say.)

COMMAND #2: Delete the previous sentence and/or paragraph. Sometimes, you may finish a sentence and realize that it needs to be deleted. Without special commands or a macro, you have to remember that the sentence needs to be deleted. This will require you to go back and reread what you wrote, which takes a lot of time. That won't do. Instead, I use the commands "delete previous sentence" and "delete previous paragraph" while I am dictating. The macro will then do just that. When combined with the Pikachu command, what remains on the page are only the sentences I meant to say. The macro deletes everything else.

COMMAND #3: Interruptions. When I dictate, I am often doing things around my house. For example, as I was dictating this very chapter, I was walking around my office. My daughter came downstairs and told me that she wanted a snack. If I were not using special commands or a macro, I would have had to pause or stop the recorder to answer her question. That's not terribly efficient.

Instead, I use the command "Bulbasaur." When I heard my daughter coming downstairs, I said the command, then kept the tape rolling. I went upstairs with the harmonica holder around my neck, fixed my daughter a snack, served her, and made sure she had everything she needed. I did all of this with the recorder still on. Then, as I walked downstairs, I said the command "Bulbasaur" again and continued this chapter where I left off. When I loaded the text into Microsoft Word, the macro identified both instances of the command "Bulbasaur." Then, it deleted the commands and everything in between—including everything I said to my daughter.

This command is a godsend when you are multitasking and can't readily push a button on your voice recorder.

This command has served me well in several scenarios, particularly when I am running errands.

- Once, I was at a drive-thru and dictating a story while I waited for the hostess to take my order. When she approached my car, I simply said, "Bulbasaur," rolled down the window, gave her my order, and paid. As soon as I rolled my window up, I said, "Bulbasaur" again and continued my story. I did the same thing when it was time to grab my food.
- When I'm washing the dishes, if my wife or daughter need something while I am dictating, my hands are usually wet. I don't want to ruin the recorder with dirty dishwater. I simply use the "Bulbasaur" command.

COMMAND #4: Lists. When I am dictating nonfiction, such as the *Indie Author Confidential* series, I frequently use ordered and unordered lists. Lists are part and parcel of nonfiction writing. When I'm ready to start a list, I simply start a new line and use the command "list item" for an ordered list and "number list item" for an unordered list. I use these commands for every line in the list. The macro will then format each line accordingly and capitalize the first letter in each line.

COMMAND #5: Insert comment. Sometimes when you're dictating, you need to remind yourself of something. Maybe your third paragraph should be the opening paragraph, or you need to remind yourself to research something. The scenarios are endless.

You know that I am committed to writing clean text correctly the first time. As a result, I don't use comments as a way to write sloppily. I use them only when I truly need them. When needed, I use the command "insert comment colon."

When I run the macro, this will create a comment and paste everything to the right of the colon into a comment box.

COMMAND #6: Style commands. I use this for bold, italic, and underlining. This command works similarly to an HTML tag. I use the command before the word or phrase I want to format.

After I've spoken that word or phrase, I say the command again. For example, I would say, "You should italic really italic try the ice cream."

The macro will then format everything between the commands (and delete the commands).

COMMAND #7: Find and replace array. In previous volumes, I talked about a Microsoft Word macro developed by Paul Beverley called FREdit. FREdit is a scripted find and replace macro that allows you to change words quickly. I got the idea to build FREdit into my dictation macro so that it automatically corrects things such as proper nouns or Dragon mishearings. For example, if I dictate the words *The Good Necromancer,* Dragon will represent the words as all lowercase. But this is a proper noun. The macro will find and replace the text accordingly. This is helpful when I mention my books or series titles. Dragon can also do this, but it's a little clunky. It's easier to update an array inside macro code (for me, at least).

As another example, I have a character in my *The Good Necromancer* series named CeCe. No matter how clearly I pronounce her name and no matter how much I train Dragon to recognize her name, it almost always transcribes her name wrong. I simply add the different variations of CeCe's name into the macro so that it will find and replace those incorrect variations for when Dragon gets it wrong. This is extremely powerful, and it is a godsend for recurring proper nouns in your story.

COMMAND #8: Sentence case and formatting for proper nouns. This was the most difficult command to solve. Proper nouns are my biggest bugbear with Dragon. It's unreasonable to expect Dragon to recognize every proper noun in the English language, but I suspect that authors spend a lot of time cleaning up proper nouns such as *Teenage Mutant Ninja Turtles, The Good Necromancer,* and so on. It's just not fun to clean up all those proper nouns.

I worked with my developer to create a sub-macro that has two parts:

1. turn proper nouns into sentence case (while keeping articles in lowercase)
2. bold, italicize, and underline those proper nouns if needed

Some proper nouns don't need to be italicized, but I wanted to build this flexibility into the macro. It wasn't easy, but we were able to figure it out. The result is that I can designate and format proper nouns in real-time as I speak.

Putting It All Together

My dictation macro makes all of my changes with the click of a button:

- I can delete incorrect sentences or paragraphs in real-time.

- I can manage interruptions with the peace of mind that they will be deleted without any effort on my part.
- I can format lists, create comments, and format the text in any way you can imagine—on the fly.
- I solved the proper noun problem.

To say this has been a game changer is an understatement. It has allowed me to dictate faster, more cleanly, and more accurately. And I spend almost no time cleaning up my transcribed text because it is accurate the first time.

Dragon still makes mistakes, though. Most of those are easily cleaned up with Microsoft's Word's Editor, Grammarly, and PerfectIt. I catch the rest as I review the text (which I already have to do anyway—no dictation session is perfect).

I am proud of this accomplishment and it has already paid dividends in helping me explode my daily word counts.

ACHIEVING NEW LEVELS OF PRODUCTIVITY

I've been thinking a lot about the impact that adopting voice recorder transcription is going to have on my productivity. In short, it is going to have a seismic impact. Honestly, I haven't truly comprehended just how seismic it is going to be.

As I was writing this book, I had a dictation session where I walked around my basement for an hour, dictating chapters from this book. I dictated 3,000 words. This is the number I dictated after applying my dictation macro. As a reminder, these words were all clean and required only minimal editing. It took less than ten minutes to edit the text and mark it as final.

That means I can dictate 3,000 words an hour on average. When I first discovered this, I thought it wasn't that much. Then I did the math and it blew me away.

To put the 3,000 words per hour in perspective, if it takes one hour to dictate 3,000 words and 10 minutes to clean up those 3,000 words, that's 70 minutes to create CLEAN, first-draft-final text.

If you do the math on an entire day's productivity, it gets really interesting.

Say you start dictating at 7 a.m. On the hour every hour, you take a 15-minute break, followed by a 15-minute clean-up session. Assuming a full workday(ish), you would dictate a total of 6 hours, which would net you 18,000 words in one day. All clean.

In a 5-day week, that would net you 90,000 words If your novels are 50,000 words, 1.8 novels.

In a month, that would net you 360,000 words, or 7.2 novels.

In a year, that would net you 4.3 million words, or 86.4 novels. I'm willing to bet you that there is a rarefied, upper echelon of writers out there doing even better than this. I write between 500,000 and 700,000 per year and am considered extremely prolific.

Now, the math looks nice, but in practice, your actual results would be far below that 4.3 million because you have a 4.3 million other things to do in your writing life, like marketing, taxes, and business.

But what if you could write even just a third of that (1.4 million words) per year? That's insane.

That's what this voice recorder and transcription have allowed me to do—get to the next levels of productivity. Or, put another way, they have helped me "level up."

Such a revelation reminds me of the importance of a few things:

1. The true question is how my editing results are. Am I accruing more errors from my editor, or is the level of editing required roughly the same? I'll know after I've produced a few books exclusively with this method.

2. I need even more refined ways of being productive. To the extent I can optimize my dictation macro, I should do so. Everything is going to depend on how

quickly and cleanly I can speak the words, lightly
edit them, and move on. If my goal is to be a first-
draft-final writer, then I need to scale my operations
accordingly.

3. I need to start doing my own covers, yesterday. You
saw the math. There is no way even the most
affluent author can afford to pay for professional
book covers for so many books.

As I become faster and more productive, I am starting to see
the upper echelons of author productivity. These are echelons I
have never seen before.

The pulp writers wrote millions of words per year… on a
typewriter. Today's authors have the benefit of technology, and
they are still mostly typing. Those who are using dictation and
transcription are probably not doing it the way I am doing it,
which means they are doing it sloppily. Or, they're spending a
fortune on human transcriptionists.

Few authors can type 3,000 words an hour for 6 hours.
That's just asking for carpal tunnel syndrome. Speaking that
much is easier; the only friction is your imagination. I've found
that my imagination does a pretty good job of keeping up with
my pace.

Therefore, I think the fastest authors writing today are using
voice recorders to achieve their speed, and they're probably
writing somewhere between five and six million words (sloppy).
I don't think annual word counts over 6 million are possible
unless you're a cyborg, but I could be wrong.

What would it mean to suddenly write several million
words per year, when I am only writing around half a million at
the time of this writing? That's profound.

When discussing my voice recorder adventures on my
YouTube channel, I encountered another author who mastered

this method and gave me some advice after expressing some hesitation with achieving such high word counts. He said, "You're right to question the power, but it's worth it."

That's a great way to think about it. Onward I go, and harness the power, I will.

AI AUDIOBOOKS: THE WATERSHED MOMENT

In 2021, Google Play opened a beta program to turn e-books into audiobooks using its AI voice technology. The goal was to take a book and have it narrated by a life-like AI.

I wasn't in the first beta, so I can't speak to how well it went, or what the quality was. Some initial comments I remember were that people thought the voices were a little too stilted. I wasn't terribly impressed with the voices myself, but the story was an interesting signal to track.

Fast-forward to today, and Google has expanded the beta. With the click of a button, Google converts your e-book to audio. If the AI narrator mispronounced a word, just click a button and teach it how to pronounce it. You can also edit the audio by editing your text; the narration will update automatically.

Google has expanded the number of voices available and also has made significant advancements in the quality of the AI narration. The advancements are significant enough that, while people were laughing at the first round of samples, they're not laughing now.

Google states that it is focused on helping authors create

audiobooks for books that probably never would have made it into audio. The company states that the best candidates (at the time of this writing) are nonfiction and other work that doesn't require much emotion in the narration. Fiction is NOT recommended.

First, let's discuss the quality of the voices because it is the least important factor in this conversation. If you know anything about AI, then you should know that it advances quickly. Successful services almost always start as laughingstocks. Then, suddenly, they're not. Remember when people laughed at Apple Maps for nearly sending people off cliffs? You don't hear stories like that anymore. Apple learned.

Now that Google opened the beta to all authors, they are now effectively training their AI models with a copious amount of data. They will have hundreds of millions of words to analyze. And with authors able to make corrections to the text, Google will be able to train its AI models much faster than previous iterations. (By the way, if you use this service, you're helping Google train their models. That's why you're getting this for free initially.)

The quality of these voices is going to make unbelievable strides now that anyone can use the tech. If quality is the only thing you are focused on, then you have missed the point, and you are in danger of missing the boat on this technology.

Quality is a red herring. What ultimately matters is convenience for the end user. In this case, the end users are authors and readers. Authors need low-cost ways to enter the audio market. The costs and barriers to entry are quite high. Readers want more books available in audio. Some readers only listen to audio. Additionally, some nonfiction readers don't really care WHO is narrating a book so long as it is engaging and gives them the information they need. For these readers, the narrator is irrelevant. If an AI reads it, so be it, as long as it doesn't sound completely mechanical.

And longer term, readers will want to be able to personalize their audiobook experience. If you want to hear a black man narrate a book, you'll be able to change the narrator with the click of a button. If you want to hear someone narrate with an Australian accent because that's what makes you comfortable, you'll be able to. That's extremely attractive.

As I said, many of the loudest voices against this technology are going to make fun of the quality. Don't fall for that. In just a few short years, those people are going to eat their words.

Next, let's talk about Google. People are skeptical of Google, and that feeling is justified. They're certainly not angels when it comes to our data. But when it comes to being the first mover of this technology, it's going to be Google, Apple, or Amazon/Audible. Take your pick. Frankly, I'm relieved Audible wasn't the first mover. This is exactly the kind of competition we need in the audiobook space.

This announcement is going to force Audible's hand. I'm positive they've been working on something similar—I'd put money on it. Now they have to do something in response to this, and that's something we should be celebrating. Healthy competition is a win for readers and a win for authors.

That brings me to the elephant in the room: narrators. It's undeniable that narrators are the biggest losers in this week's announcement.

Narrators are right to be concerned about what a technology like this will do to their livelihoods. I'm not cheering for the destruction of their profession, and I certainly don't want the narrators I've worked with to be out of a job as a result of this technology. But there's also not much any of us can do about it. Trying to stop this technology is like standing on the beach, trying to beat up the ocean. Anyone who thinks they can stop its advancement is delusional. I don't believe that this tech is going to eliminate narrators completely. There will always be readers who want a human narrator, just like there will always be readers who prefer paperbacks.

Trying to pretend reader tastes aren't changing and/or trying to stop it from happening is not productive. Narrators will have to find ways to shift their skillset to compensate for the impending changes. I don't like that any more than the next person, but I think the sooner people accept that change is coming, the faster they'll be able to find a solution that helps them move forward.

That brings me to something I've seen some people say about Google auto-narration (and AI narration in general) that is headshakingly stupid and misinformed. The statement goes something like this: "We can't let Google/Amazon/whoever flood the market with a tsunami of crap!"

Remember my comments on quality. Also, I don't consider myself a self-publishing historian because I haven't been doing this nearly as long as others, but...the words "tsunami of crap/flood of garbage/etc." should have special meaning for indies.

I recall a time not too long ago when people made that very argument against self-published books. Ten years ago, I remember people saying to my face that self-publishing was garbage—why would I even think about it? They begged me to sign with a publisher to save my career. (These people, by the way, had never published a book.)

I remember the Kindle gold rush. I was working on my first book when it happened. I remember the bitter debates people had about the "value" of traditional publishers. If you think the debate between traditional and self-publishing now is bad, you have no idea how vociferous it was ten years ago.

Anyway, my point is that I remember too vividly the battles

that people like me and other seasoned authors in this space had to fight to blaze this path. I haven't heard the words "tsunami of crap" in a long time, and now it's coming back again, this time from authors and narrators who have no understanding of recent history or technology.

If you're an indie author uttering these words, shame on you. You wouldn't be publishing if it weren't for that "tsunami of crap." If all those people who hated self-published authors had their way 10 to 15 years ago with the advent of the Kindle (which by the way, wasn't warmly received by many in the industry at first either), then you'd be signed with a publisher and miserable...if you got published at all. Or worse, you'd be lamenting the fact that you paid a vanity publisher and have stacks of books in your garage that no one will buy.

If you're a narrator uttering those words, I understand the pain. Still, many narrators today wouldn't be where they are if it weren't for that self-publishing "tsunami of crap" back in the day. Because that's just it—the "tsunami of crap" wasn't actually crap. Sure, some of it was. But while critics were busy pointing out the crap, many, many GREAT authors, narrators, and free-lancers were able to make a living. Many of these people who would not be where they are today if it weren't for the advent of self-publishing.

What critics failed to understand in the early days of self-publishing was that it was actually a tsunami of opportunity. Those who recognized it early have amazing success to show for it. Those who did not eventually came around to the status quo. Or, they're no longer around.

So, I hope detractors of this new AI technology dispense with the "tsunami of crap" line of reasoning because it's not a good look. It's hypocritical at best and disingenuous at worst. Any time people start romanticizing the way they do business, that's never a good sign. Your alarm bells should go off and you should immediately question everything you hear. You should also be skeptical of anyone in the indie space trying to "stop a tsunami of crap." Again, it shows no understanding of recent history.

As this technology heats up and the voices start getting loud, the most important thing you can do is make decisions based on logic, not emotion. The plain fact about AI narration is that it's here, and now it's here in a big way. You can choose to embrace it or reject it.

Unfortunately, the universe doesn't care what you decide. Even if Google fails at this endeavor, the bell has been rung at this point...

My recommendation is to do your own research, validate it with your own experience, and ignore the loudest voices—both opponents AND proponents. As with all things, the truth is usually in the middle.

Now, let's talk about Google again. I spent some time playing around with the technology. The quality of the voices is much, much better than I expected. I would reserve any judgment on the voice quality until you've heard real results. They're shockingly good. I converted one of my books, *Indie Author Confidential Vol. 1* into AI audio, and the results were very good.

It's clear Google has been working on this for a while, and the product development is on-point. The problem with Google is that they don't always commit to its products. But if they stay committed to this one, it's a game changer.

The product has still has some rough edges. There are still moments where you definitely know you're listening to a bot. But, honestly, in the audiobooks I produced, I would say that the recordings were 90 to 95 percent perfect. I only had to make minor corrections here and there. No one is going to be fooled that this is *not* an AI, but that's not the point. The point is that the AI is pleasant to listen to. It'll only get better.

If Google can figure out ways to make the editing just a little faster, and if they keep improving the quality of the voices, we're probably 5 to 7 years away from viable fiction AI narration, maybe sooner. And then everything will change.

I didn't think Google would be the one to make the first move, and I believe this is the watershed moment that people have been waiting for. It's hard not to see Audible and/or Spotify making a move into AI narration after this.

Also, I should also point out that I reviewed Google Play's auto-narration terms of service, and I didn't see anything unusual at first glance. No rights grabs, no funny business, or no unclear language. Yet.

Google also gives you the ability to sell the audio on your own website as long as the audiobook is for sale on Google Play. That's pretty generous. I think readers will initially be skeptical, but they'll be pretty quick to embrace this technology, especially if authors price their audiobook editions correctly.

I believe in the technology so much that I produced AI audio editions of the entire *Indie Author Confidential* series. Moving forward, AI audio will be a launch format for new entries in the series.

I don't know for sure, but AI audio now feels like self-publishing did in 2011 and 2012. That's an exciting feeling. It's going to be a little messy at first, but if history is any indication, the first movers will reap the biggest advantages.

I think we're in for a crazy ride in the audio space.

PORTFOLIO MANAGEMENT ACHIEVEMENTS

I have talked at length about portfolio management and how important it is in my long-term strategy of being a world-class content creator, technology and data-driven writer, and writer of the future. When you have as much intellectual property as I do, you have to develop a way to manage your work quickly, effectively, and with the same agility as an author who only has a few books. This sounds somewhat counterintuitive, but I have proven that it can be done.

My master publishing file is how I am accomplishing this agility. My master publishing file is an Excel spreadsheet that contains all the metadata for my books. You name it, it's there: title, subtitle, series title, ISBNs, links to retailers, and so on. It sounds simple—and it is—but it's amazing how many people don't have all of this information in one place at their fingertips. They often have to go hunting for it. I don't.

I made some improvements to my master publishing file this quarter that will be beneficial for me in the long run.

First, I performed "deep checks" for a subset of my books this quarter. A deep check involves reviewing all sales pages at all retailers as well as how the book is set up on retailer dashboards, looking for anything wrong. A deep check takes approximately 30 minutes per book, and it is a failsafe to ensure that nothing is terribly wrong. I make sure the right version of the book is published, that the right version is for sale, that it has the most up-to-date book description, and so on.

Next, I updated the file to include links for my books on Barnes & Noble. I have neglected Barnes & Noble for a long time, and they are still not a major part of my distribution strategy. However, when I schedule promotions, many of the venues want a Barnes & Noble link. This prompted me to add Barnes & Noble links for all of my books to the master publishing file. This took approximately two hours, but I don't have to worry about hunting for those links anymore.

Next, I reduced the number of hyperlinks in my e-books. At the beginning of my career, I was a little too undisciplined with how I handled hyperlinks. I did foolish things with links in my books.

- I linked to book sales pages on other retailers. Not only is this a no-no, but it also doesn't age well.
- I linked to podcast episodes. This is unwise because if the podcast host stops paying for their show, it becomes unlisted. Therefore, your links become obsolete overnight (and you won't even know).
- I included affiliate links to products on Amazon. This is foolish because products go off sale all the time on Amazon, especially when there is a new version of that product. Therefore, my affiliate links were sending people to invalid product pages and/or obsolete products.

In reviewing my link strategy, some things didn't make sense anymore, like including a million links on my author biography page. I streamlined that.

I also reduced the number of links on my copyright page. I used to link to my cover designers' websites, but I stopped doing that because I realized that if my cover designer goes out of business or stops accepting work, the website could become invalid. Instead, I just mention their names. It's far more evergreen.

I updated the interiors for all of my books and reduced the number of links by anywhere from 80 to 90 percent. This made a big difference in the evergreen potential and professionalism of my books.

As I mentioned in a previous volume in this series, I created a master link log that contains all the links in all of my books with an Excel macro that checks whether the links are valid. Every time I publish a new book, I used Calibre to export all the links in the book into an Excel file that I combine with my master link log with minimal effort. Then, on January 1 of each year, I have a calendar reminder set to run my master link log macro. In just a few minutes, I know if there are any broken links in my books. If I run the master link log at 8 a.m., I can have changes identified and published at all retailers by 8:30 a.m. For *all* of my books. That's what I'm talking about when I talk about agility and being nimble. I can catch and fix broken links quickly and fix them quickly.

I also discovered a problem with my e-book files. In Vellum, I was not using store-specific exports. Vellum allows you to export a different EPUB file optimized for each of the major retailers (Amazon, Apple, Google, Kobo, and so on). When I first started using Vellum, I disabled this feature because I only wanted to worry about one EPUB file. I discovered that this was a mistake. For starters, it was causing the "look inside" samples on Amazon to be improperly formatted. When readers would preview the book, the background would be blue. (When they purchased the book, everything looked fine, but the sample suggested that I didn't know how to format my books. Oddly enough, this didn't happen for all of my books, but it happened for enough of them that it was a problem.) I believe this could have cost me some sales. Fortunately, readers never said anything about it, but it bothered me to have this type of quality error.

At the same time I reduced the number of links in my books, I also regenerated my books to include store-specific exports from Vellum. I then re-uploaded these new versions of all of my books, followed up a few days later to make sure the correct versions were published and available, and I updated my master publishing file accordingly.

This was a colossal amount of work, but it now ensures that my books are compliant with all book retailers and (hopefully) look good on a broader range of devices now.

I also took the opportunity to improve my pricing on Google Play. Google Play's interface used to be pretty bad. In fact, I would argue that it was one of the worst publishing interfaces in the industry. They've come a long way.

When I first published my books on Google Play, setting a price was a hassle. It was counterintuitive and overly difficult. When Google Play updated the Google Play dashboard, it made setting book prices much easier (in addition to moving to an agency pricing model, which was a welcome improvement).

When I began using the new dashboard, I segmented my pricing so that the major currencies were priced appropriately: US dollars, British pounds, euros, Australian dollars, and Canadian dollars. However, my earlier books did not have this level of pricing segmentation. I had set the US dollar price and then let the system convert the price to other currencies automatically. That is never a good idea when you can help it.

I still am not a fan of Google Play's pricing segmentation. I feel that it is too many mouse clicks and you shouldn't have to choose which currencies you want to set pricing. They should make it easier to set currencies more quickly like their competitors. But, it is what it is. I set aside an afternoon to go through my older books and segment the prices accordingly. This will make my entire portfolio more attractive to Google Play readers all over the world.

Amazon also introduced further pricing segmentation for Poland and Sweden. I set aside another afternoon to update my book prices in these currencies to make them more attractive to readers in those markets.

Payhip also introduced a feature where you can segment your product into different formats. Previously, if I wanted to sell the e-book and audiobook on my website, I had to create two different products with two different links. Now, I can create one product that has an e-book version, an audiobook version, and a combined version. I went through my portfolio and updated the products that could benefit from this more sophisticated format segmentation.

And last but not least, Google Play introduced a new AI audiobook tool that I discussed in a previous chapter. I developed the entire *Indie Author Confidential* series into audio within a couple of weeks. That broadened my reach for this series and made it available to more readers. Plus, I could also sell the AI audiobook versions on my website.

Those are my portfolio management achievements this quarter.

SPEAKING ENGAGEMENT SUCCESS

I attended my first in-person speaking engagement since 2018.

My, how the world has changed. It was great to be among writers again in-person. I attended Inkers Con in Dallas, Texas, and the annual Writer's Digest Conference in New York City in Midtown. Both events were great.

Now that I am back on the conference circuit again, I have taken some actions to make it easier to prepare for speaking events.

First, I now think twice about any speaking engagement that is not directly tied to one of my books. If I wrote a book about it, I can speak about it, and that cuts my preparation time in half. Otherwise, I will need to start from scratch, which will require a higher fee. This has allowed me to build a bank of presentations that I can recycle in the future. This is more efficient, and it saves me money while also providing good credibility to the organizer. Organizers like to see presentations ahead of time; it shows them that you are prepared and gives them a taste of what to expect for their event.

Second, I developed a new presentation template. I purchased a premium PowerPoint template from a design website. The slides are professionally designed, easy to customize, and visually stunning without being over the top. This will be my new template for the next few years. This way, everything will be branded and consistent.

Third, I adopted a sales technique I observed one speaker do. It was so smooth and effortless that I wondered why I had never thought of it.

The technique was as follows:

- At the end of the presentation, the speaker concluded the slide deck with a question slide that contained a QR code.
- The QR code took participants to a sales page on the speaker's website that contained an image of the speaker waving from a recognizable landmark at the hotel the conference was in, which was a great personal touch. It also included a link to the PowerPoint presentation, a few other bonuses, and a button to schedule a consultation with a discount.

I thought this was brilliant. I implemented this same strategy and it worked extremely well. The only thing I will change is the administration of the QR code. I found that many participants loved the fact that I offered a QR code, but it wasn't the easiest thing to manage on a smartphone internet browser when you only have a few minutes. What I should have done was created a printout on premium card stock with images of myself, my book, the link, and the QR code. This way, participants could scan the code in their own time and engage with the content without worrying about having to run off to the next speech at the conference. Including the link on the card would have also been helpful for people accessing the sales page on their desktop computers. In other words, everyone wins.

I also had some setbacks. Both times I traveled, my return flight was either delayed or canceled. I had to spend the night in Dallas because the last flight to my city for the day was canceled. Then, when I got to O'Hare Airport in Chicago, my flight was delayed. I spent eight hours at O'Hare Airport.

My trip home from New York City wasn't much better. I was also stranded at O'Hare airport for four hours (when I was only supposed to be there for one).

The current economic climate has wreaked havoc on airlines (actually, the airlines did this to themselves, but I digress). The result is that traveling is significantly more difficult than it used to be. I don't see this ending anytime soon. As someone who enjoys speaking but has a full-time job, this is problematic for me because I have to take off work to attend a speaking event. Therefore, I have decided to be more deliberate in the speaking engagements I take on.

For every event I attend, there is an opportunity cost. I have to spend time preparing for the event, traveling to and from, being at the event, and catching up when I return. This cost for me is worth it, but the unpleasantries of traveling right now and the fact that I live in a city that is hard to get in and out of makes me have to think twice about in-person invitations for the foreseeable future. That's not a bad thing. Ultimately, I feel it was good to have these bad airport experiences because they made me realize the importance of discipline.

Anyway, it feels good to be back at in-person events.

THE IDEA WELL

I thought it would be fun (and helpful for me) to start a new recurring segment in this series. I'm calling it the Idea Well, and it will contain inspirations and influences that made it into the books I wrote for that quarter. This will be a useful way for me to reflect on where my ideas came from, and it could be a fun Easter egg for fans of my work.

Year of the Rat (The Chicago Rat Shifter, Book 3)

This is the third and final book in my urban fantasy series about a protagonist who can shift into a rat. He is turned into a rat against his will, and since Chicago is one of the rattiest cities in the world, he's in good company.

Chicago features prominently in this series. I've always believed that the setting is a character in urban fantasy. I sprinkled little Chicago references throughout the series, but the most prominent are the epigraphs that I start each book with. The epigraphs are taken from the *Spoon River Anthology* by Edgar Lee Masters. Masters' poetry captures the spirit of life in Illinois in the late nineteenth century. Masters also spent time in Chicago as a practicing lawyer, and he was inducted into the Chicago Literary Hall of Fame in 2014. His poetry is free verse that expresses the epitaphs of different people who live in the fictional town of Spoon River. I read his poetry in college and was always taken by it. He has such a way of capturing the human spirit. Because his work is now in the public domain, I was free to use it in my novels.

The epigraphs (which are epitaphs) mirror the villains. They could be narrated by the villain themselves and encompass the villain's theme. Book 1 is about being drawn toward someone who doesn't love you; Book 2 is about stunted growth and living with death (the villain is a necromancer); Book 3 is about the cruelty of life. Again, the themes match not only the story but also the villain's aesthetic. Ironically, this was purely a coincidence that I didn't realize until I wrote this chapter.

In *Year of the Rat*, the villain is a hardscrabble demon collector who stores his collection of evil beings in the bodies of willing servants. He's stuck in the 1970s, is high on weed for most of the novel, and has an affinity for mink coats. He's the kind of guy who goes bump in the night, and not the kind at all you want to mess with. Some of his scenes were terrifying to write.

His name is JoJo Skaggs. He was inspired by a great song called "JoJo" by Boz Scaggs. The first line of the song is "Look out behind you, JoJo's got his gun."

In JoJo's first scene, he pulls a gun on his bartender, who is snooping around the back office of JoJo's nightclub. He jams the gun in the bartender's back, who can't turn around or he'll get shot. That's an homage to that infamous song lyric.

JoJo has a down-on-her-luck girlfriend named Simone, whose name is taken from a song called "Simone" on Boz Scaggs's *Middle Man* album, the same album that contains the song "JoJo." I always like to find ways to pay tribute to great musicians in my work. *Year of the Rat* continues this tradition.

I also discovered another interesting piece of Chicago history while writing the book. In the late 1800s and early 1900s, there were underground freight tunnels in downtown Chicago that were used to transport trash and merchandise between the buildings downtown. These tunnels had little trains that ran through them daily. It's a fascinating piece of history and testament to what an amazing architectural wonder the city of Chicago is. (Frankly, it is a miracle the city even exists, but that's another topic.)

Those tunnels are the fodder of fiction. The inner writer in me couldn't help but weave this piece of history into *The Chicago Rat Shifter*. In the novel, my hero, Cyrus, encounters a clan of gnomes who are protectors of the earth that dwell underneath the city.

There are many more inspirations that made their way into *Year of the Rat*, but those are the most prominent.

BECOME A TECHNOLOGY
AND DATA-DRIVEN WRITER

LESSONS IN COVER DESIGN THIS QUARTER

I took some meaningful steps this quarter to position myself to learn the art of cover design. I'm still behind where I want to be, but I am making progress.

The current inflation crisis is a constant reminder for me that I need to get moving on this. I anticipate that cover designers will raise their rates again soon. Why wouldn't they? Inflation is crazy right now.

In the previous section, I talked at length about my adventures with voice recording, dictation, and transcription. I have paved the groundwork to start accruing words in a significantly faster manner than I ever have in my writing. If I'm going to do that, I *must* start designing my own covers. I simply don't have a choice, especially if I write more than 20 books per year, and especially if inflation continues (which it will).

Next, I had an illustrated cover done for *Year of the Rat*, and while I liked the cover, it's another reminder that I need to find a more sustainable way to handle my cover design.

Finally, I obtained a mentor who is quite adept at cover design. I can now ask him any question I want about design, and he has graciously agreed to help me build a branded cover template. He also agreed to look at any covers I create. Having him in my back pocket will be critical as I begin learning.

Again, this is a short chapter, but it is my way of holding myself accountable for the steps I've taken. It is also my way of showing that I am beginning to walk the walk and put my money where my mouth is.

BUILDING AN EASIER MASTER
PUBLISHING FILE

Google Play announced enhancements to its publishing dashboard this year. The enhancements are mostly visual and are aimed at making it easier to use their platform.

Google made it easier for authors to use its batch upload feature. Google Play, PublishDrive, and StreetLib are the only retailers I know of that allow for bulk uploading and changes. For example, if you want to upload ten books at the same time, or make changes to those ten books at the same time, these retailers provide an Excel spreadsheet template that you can use to facilitate the changes more economically. Unfortunately, each retailer has three different spreadsheets, but you get the picture.

(On a slightly related note, publishers make bulk changes using the ONIX standard; I've talked about it at length in previous volumes of this series. It's possible for indies, but too technical for most people).

Google has offered bulk uploading changes for a long time; they just make it easier now.

Google now provides a spreadsheet that you can download that contains the metadata for all of your books. I think you had to request this in the past. When I say they provide everything, I mean they provide *everything*. If you want a shortcut to building a master publishing file, then just use Google's template. They've done all the hard work for you. Hell, if I hadn't built a master publishing file, then I would definitely have used Google's. It's a great start, and you can add other columns as needed. This would have saved me a lot of time in 2021.

I'm just passing this tip along.

AUDIOBOOK PROOFING WITH AI SOFTWARE

I produced audiobook versions of *The Author Estate Handbook* and *The Author Heir Handbook*. I hired a professional narrator to do the job.

We followed the typical audiobook production process, which is as follows:

1. I provided a list of proper noun pronunciations for any words that might not be immediately obvious.
2. The narrator provided a sample for me to review and comment on.
3. The narrator then recorded the entire book and sent me all the audio files upon completion.
4. I listened to the audio and provided feedback.

However, I did something different this time that was a follow-up on a chapter that I wrote in a previous volume in the series. The idea was to use a proofreader for the audiobook.

Over the past few years, I have encountered individuals who listen to audiobooks, compare the audio with the text, and provide a summary of any differences, mispronunciations, or formatting errors, such as missing sentences. I thought this was a great idea, and I promised to hire an audio proofreader the next time I produced an audiobook.

Fortunately, they aren't hard to find. I found one on Fiverr. I sent the proofer the audio files with detailed instructions on what I wanted her to look for; one week later, she sent me a report with everything wrong with the audio. This freed me up to simply listen to the audio for major issues without having to do the tedious work of comparing the audio to the text. I sent that report to the narrator, who made corrections, and I performed the final listen-through of the book to make sure that the changes were made correctly.

I am not a big fan of "waving away" my responsibilities. Just because I'm not doing the work doesn't mean that I ignore my proofer's work product. I checked the proofreader's work to make sure she did a good job, and she did.

Another tool that I used in this process to ensure higher quality was Pozotron. Pozotron is also a service that I covered in a previous volume of this series; it is an automated audiobook proofreading software that uses artificial intelligence to catch errors. It scans your audio, compares it to the text, and flags any discrepancies. It works quite well.

For *The Author Heir Handbook*, I trained the audiobook proofer to use Pozotron. I granted her access to the project, and she went through and reviewed the discrepancies as well as performed a customary listen and proofread of the audio. The result was outstanding. The narrator and I both felt that we had eliminated almost all errors with the first draft of his narration.

Moving forward, when I produce audiobooks, I will let the proofing software and the human proofer do the tedious work, then I will follow up as the last line of quality defense. This process, while adding two extra steps, increases the quality of the audiobook production.

FIXING A MISTAKE IN A LIVE
AUDIOBOOK

After I published the audiobook version of *The Author Estate Handbook,* I caught an error that the narrator and I both missed. (I did not use Pozotron for this book. If I had, it would have most definitely caught this problem.)

The error was relatively simple. There were a few paragraphs that didn't belong in one of the chapters. It would have made the listener tilt their head for a few seconds, but it was a relatively minor offense.

I did not want to inconvenience my narrator, so I figured out if I could fix the problem myself.

It helps tremendously that I produced my own audiobook four *150 Self-Publishing Questions Answered,* so I know the technical parts of audio production. I also know the problems that narrators run into when submitting audio for quality check.

The fix was as easy as loading the MP3 of the chapter in question, cutting out the unnecessary paragraphs, making sure that the "tail" of the audio met audiobook retailer standards, and re-exporting the file with the proper specifications. I have a free audio editing software called Audacity that has a plug-in called ACX Check. ACX Check scans your audio to determine whether it is compliant with Audible's technical specifications. If it's not, it will tell you why. Fortunately, the file passed ACX Check.

I re-uploaded the audio to Audible and Findaway Voices. Within a week, the new changes were published and live. I sent an email to the narrator afterward with a summary of what I changed and asked him to make the change when he had an opportunity.

Why would I email my narrator to tell him this? When I licensed my estate planning books to ALLi, I told them that I would review the books in three years to determine whether anything was obsolete, and I committed to keeping the books up-to-date. This means that I must also keep the audiobooks up-to-date. And to do that, it means that the narrator and I must stay in sync. When I engage him in 2025, I am going to have to give him a list of edits and timestamps. If those are off by even just a few seconds, it will cause massive confusion.

Thank goodness I was organized and technical enough to solve this problem. It saved me some time and money, and my narrator was grateful that he did not have to stop what he was doing to help me out.

BULK FILE RENAMING

In the previous section, I discussed Google Play's new AI audiobook feature and how it is a watershed moment in the audiobook world.

Google allows you to download the audiobook files so that you can sell them in other places, such as your website. However, when they give you the files, the metadata on the files is blank. The only thing Google does for you is number your chapters. That's not helpful for anybody!

If you want to manage your audiobook properly, you need to know which file represents which chapter; you also need to have complete metadata so that when you upload your file somewhere (or someone downloads your files onto their device), they know what they're listening to. This was a major oversight on Google's part.

Fortunately, there are apps to help with this problem.

Here's what most people would do: they would manually change the file names and the metadata by themselves (if they did it at all). This is time-consuming and laborious.

Here's how to handle this problem using technology, data,

and automation. It requires several steps, but it will produce good results.

First, the important thing is to remember that problems like this are data problems, not effort problems. When you think about your metadata and audio files as *data*, you will think about this differently.

Ultimately, your audiobook files are a giant block of data.

I found a Windows application that allows you to create a comma-separated value (CSV) file with the old file names in one column and your desired file names in the second column. That begs the question of how you can get your chapter names into Excel. The answer is no, you don't type them in.

Calibre has a feature that allows you to export the table of contents as a CSV file. You can then take the data from that file and paste it into your Excel template in just a few seconds.

Once you set up the Excel file properly, the Windows application will change all of your file names in seconds.

That solves the file name problem. But we still have to solve the metadata problem.

If you have ever looked at the metadata of an MP3, it is stored in what is called an ID3 tag. An ID3 tag contains all the information anyone would ever want to know about a file: track title, artist, album, album artist, track number, cover, and more. ID3 tag editors are easy to find, and they are often free. Many can edit your ID3 tags in bulk.

I found a cheap ID3 tag editor that allowed me to import the audiobook files (with fresh new file names) and edit the tags for all the files at the same time. The metadata looks something like this:

- Album: *Indie Author Confidential: Vol. 10*
- Artist: M.L. Ronn
- Album artist: M.L. Ronn

- Year: 2022

I was able to update all the files with this metadata in just a few seconds. I was also able to create another Excel template that imported the file names as track titles. Lastly, the editor allowed me to apply track numbers so that all the files would be loaded sequentially when the reader opens them in the app of their choice.

When I was done, I had audiobook files with clean file names and metadata. The overall process took approximately five minutes, which is much faster than someone doing this manually. I repeated this process for every AI audiobook in the *Indie Author Confidential* series, and I will continue to use this process for every AI audiobook that I create until Google develops a fix for this problem.

This is yet another example of how understanding data allows you to do things in minutes that would take other people hours. This is why understanding data is a critical advantage for every author in today's digital world.

CLIPBOARD MANAGER

I don't remember how I heard about clipboard managers. Maybe I saw a video for one on YouTube; maybe someone told me about them—it's fuzzy now, but boy, am I so glad that I stumbled upon them.

A clipboard manager is an application that stores everything that you copy to the clipboard. It functions similarly to a word processor storing every instance of undo and redo. The only difference is that you can recall everything you have ever copied to the clipboard.

Why would you want an application like this, you ask?

Let me count the ways that clipboard managers can be extremely useful:

- when you have to paste the same data over and over again. I scheduled an ad stacking campaign earlier this year and found myself having to input the same links, ISBNs, and other items that required so much time and effort to hunt down.

- when you paste something, copy something else to your clipboard, and need to recall the original pasted item quickly without searching for it.
- when you copy something and would have otherwise lost it if you couldn't recall it.

With a quick keyboard shortcut, I can pull up everything I have ever copied to my clipboard. I can even save favorite copied items. It is amazing. I can't tell you how much time it has saved me and my everyday operations. The app I bought was surprisingly affordable too.

Anyway, I strongly recommend clipboard managers. I don't know how I ever lived without one.

AUTOMATING REVIEWS

I recently had a service done at my house. A few hours after the service person left my home, I received a text message with a request for a review and a link. The link took me to a screen that gave me the choice of leaving a review on Google, Facebook, the Better Business Bureau, the company's website, and a few other places. I left a review on the platform of my choice. It was very easy and I only had to sign into my account for that platform. The entire process took two minutes.

This is the sort of thing I dream about as an author. How grand would it be to send an email to a reader with a link to leave a review on their retailer of choice? It would make gathering reviews a breeze!

I found a way to *kind of* do this with Genius Links. You can build a Genius Link Choice Page that contains logos and links to all the retailers you want people to leave reviews to, and you can use special links that take readers directly to the review page for a given book. However, it does have some downsides and it doesn't function nearly as smoothly as what I just described above.

The best application for this would be for direct sales—if

someone buys one of my books, an autoresponder could send the reader to the review page for that book.

The only difference between homeowners and readers is that homeowners have had the service performed and it will be fresh on their minds; readers may not read a book right away, so a request for a review would be annoying. This is where I think retailers could step in to solve this problem, but they don't seem to be terribly interested in it.

That said, this was a great customer experience, and I hope indie authors can get something like it someday because it would be a game changer.

LESSONS IN FACEBOOK ADS

While at Inkers Con in Dallas, I attended a session on Facebook Ads. I sat next to an extremely successful romance author who gave me some pointers after the talk. The chat, which lasted five minutes, left me feeling enthusiastic about finally getting around to Facebook Ads. I made a promise to myself at the conference that I would make my very first Facebook Ad before I got on the plane to go home.

Well, I would have broken that promise to myself because I ended up being preoccupied with conference activities on the last night. Suddenly, I found myself sitting on the plane with no Facebook Ads to my name. Imagine my surprise when the pilot came on the intercom and announced that the flight was canceled due to a maintenance issue with the airplane.

Everyone had to get off the plane, and I couldn't find another flight home until the next morning. I had to stay at a hotel.

Sitting in the hotel room, I realized that this had to be a sign from the universe. It kept me from breaking that promise to myself. I spent the rest of the night learning about Facebook Ads, and I made not one, but two ads before I went to bed.

Upon arriving home, I discovered that the ads were complete disasters, but they did give me some valuable data that I was able to use to improve my next ad. One week later, my ads were profitable! That month became the best sales month ever in the history of my writing business. My sales increased and have not dropped to pre-Facebook Ad levels since.

It's funny how the universe works sometimes. I could have bitched and moaned about being stuck in Dallas for an extra night. I could've taken my wrath out on American Airlines, an airline that I will never fly on again, even if it's a cold day in hell. But instead, I kept my eyes on the publishing business, and it was one of the best successes I enjoyed this year.

Am I perfect at Facebook Ads? No. I've run a lot of ads that haven't done well since. But a lot of them have, and that's something to be grateful for.

ANOTHER WAY TO RUN
AMAZON ADS

I've been running Amazon Ads since 2017. In the beginning, I had middling success with them. It wasn't enough to keep them going.

I decided to invest in a premium course in 2018. That taught me the ins and outs of the platform. I quickly recovered the money I made on the course in a very short time, and my Amazon Ads have not produced a loss for me since 2019.

The school of thought of the course I purchased a few years ago was to never trust the Amazon dashboard. Amazon is slow to report data, and the data they report is not always complete. Therefore, you don't really know how effective your ads are.

Lately, I've been coming across people who are vehemently disagreeing with that school of thought. They argue that no, the Amazon dashboard is *very* accurate. It is slow, but only by about 14 days. If your dashboard says that you're taking a loss, then you're taking a loss. This school of thought is adamant that the other school of thought is full of scammers. After all, it's awfully convenient for an ad guru to say that the ad dashboards don't work so that you can't hold them accountable for poor results. If your results are good, they may not actually be because of the instructors' advice because—well, you can't trust the data. This school takes a different tactical approach to ads, bidding high on a small subset of target products instead of a shotgun approach that the first school advocates for.

I believe both schools have some merits. The first school is valuable because it has gotten many people comfortable with the ad platform. The second approach is valuable because it teaches people to think with their heads, not their hearts.

I tried both methods, and I can't definitively say that one is better than the other. I think they both have their time and place.

What I can say is that the answer is probably somewhere in the middle. We should probably give Amazon's data more credibility than the first school does, but we shouldn't rule out the fact that a decent amount of book sales could be coming from sources other than the ads.

It goes to show you that there isn't just one way to do anything in this business.

REEVALUATING CURRENCY
EXCHANGE RATES

The euro is heavy on my mind. Recent reports have shown the value of the currency being 1:1 with the US dollar.

This means that collectively, a book sale in a euro country is worth less than it was two years ago if you're an American like me. I historically benefited when Europeans bought my books because of strong currency exchange rates.

I'm going to meander for the next few paragraphs, but there is a point at the end.

I've talked many times about how I created Excel macros that slice and dice my sales reports into a nice database that I can run reports from.

One component of these Excel macros is currency conversions. Every retailer except Amazon does currency conversions for you, and you don't even have to think about it when you look at their sales reports.

Amazon is a pain in this regard because its detailed sales reports don't tell you what you actually got paid in your home currency when you sell books in foreign stores. For example, if I sell a €4.99 book in Germany, the report will tell me that I made approximately €3.45, not what I made in dollars. To get the dollar amount, I need to look at a separate monthly payment report that includes a German exchange rate factor. Then I must multiply the commission by that factor to get the actual amount I got paid. And even then, because of rounding, it'll never be 100. But it will be close.

Also, Amazon's bank uses different exchange rates than any other bank I've tracked, so you can't do this math with publicly available exchange rates. If you do, your numbers will be way, way off.

Amazon could solve this problem once and forever by simply including the exchange rates on the detailed royalty report and then do the math for you. But alas...I have to do it with an Excel macro instead.

If you don't account for exchange rates on Amazon, then you will never have accurate sales figures. There is one very prominent sales tracker on the market that, last I tested, did NOT do this math. It doesn't even convert the currencies. It's headshakingly bad. But I digress.

Anyway, my Amazon sales report macro does this math by estimating the past 6-year average of the Amazon bank's exchange rate between 2014 and 2020 for every month I got paid during that period, and then it applies that factor to my foreign royalty amount to get an accurate conversion and estimate of what I made in any given month. Because exchange rates fluctuate over time, you're better to use an average. In my tests, my currency conversions got me to within 90 to 95 percent of what I actually made, and my numbers were just as accurate if not more than Book Report, a prominent sales tracker on the market right now.

Anyway, maybe you don't care about that. Maybe you never thought about it. But I do because I want my database of sales to always be accurate and up-to-date. I know to the penny of what I made for every book in every country in every format, and I can get those numbers in just a few minutes. Very, very powerful, and unlike some people who use sales trackers with browser extensions, my data is private.

With the falling euro exchange rates, I think it's time for me to go in and redo the math on my euro factors. They're current through 2020. For Germany, the Netherlands, Italy, and Spain, the average exchange rate was about 1.12. This means that a €4.99 book at a 70 percent royalty would net me about $3.86 (3.45 x 1.12). In France, the historical exchange rate has been a little better at 1.68, which would net a $5.79 royalty.

With current exchange rates, if it's true that the euro and dollar are close to 1:1, then that means that the same sale would now be $3.45 (everywhere but France), which is objectively worse in all euro countries. But again, I need to review Amazon's exchange rates to see just how bad it is.

Honestly, I probably need to do this exercise for all my currencies again by adding the last 24 months into my current average. It would strengthen my factors from 60 months to 84 months and therefore lead to better and more accurate conversions when I slice and dice my reports into my database.

I think the wrong thing to do right now is to raise my euro prices. I'll probably wait until the war in Ukraine ends, assuming it ends soon. Otherwise, if you raise your prices and the exchange rates rally, you'll shoot yourself in the foot. Plus, people raising their prices is what leads to more inflation. That's ultimately bad for readers.

This is the kind of stuff I sit around and think about when I have spare time and am procrastinating on a novel...

SELLING ENTIRE BIBLIOGRAPHIES
OF MY WORK

I was looking for some music to listen to, and I stumbled upon Bandcamp. I have been a Bandcamp listener since 2010, and I know I can always find good music there. Bandcamp has a feature that allows you to purchase an artist's entire discography for a discounted price. I have done this in the past for artists whose work I love. For a good price (or a price that I choose), I can support an artist and get lots of great music to add to my library.

This got me thinking about how to accomplish something similar on my direct sales platform.

There's no denying that being able to offer your entire bibliography to your truest fans is a beautiful thing. It is even more beautiful if you give them additional bonuses that they can't find elsewhere.

It's a great idea, but there are some logistic issues. Let's talk through them.

When you upload the books to your direct sales platform, you would have to do it as a ZIP file unless the platform uses technology to make this easier.

Assuming that you would have to do this manually, you

would have to maintain a master file that contains the most up-to-date versions of all of your books. If you update one of your books, you will also have to update this master file and re-upload it to your direct sales platform. This requires extreme organization, and it would be time-consuming.

Next, let's say that a reader does buy your entire bibliography. If they buy it on January 1, by December, you will have added more books to that bibliography. Does the reader get the new books? Probably not. But how will they know that the new books exist? How could they update their bibliography if they wanted to? In other words, if someone purchased all of your books once, and then want to do it again, how easy would it be for them to do that?

Those are the major issues I see with this sales technique. Technically, you could hire a developer to create a PowerShell or AppleScript that could grab the requisite files from all your book folders and compile them into a master file. Anytime you want to recompile the directory, just run the script. This is doable.

Another way around this problem could be to sell bundles of your work from certain periods. For example, you could structure your bibliography much like a poet structures multiple collected works. You could do a bibliography from 2010 to 2015, 2016 to 2020, and so on. This way, readers always know where they are in the bibliography. You just have to release a new bibliography every few years. Is it still clunky? Yes, but with the right finesse, it could be accomplished.

This is yet another technology that I hope makes its way to the author world one day. It would allow authors with decent platforms to make meaningful money and serve their fans.

LOOKING FORWARD

A PERSONAL TRIAL

Through 2022, I endured a personal trial unlike anything I have experienced in my life. It took me away from writing for a time, and it was life-changing for me and my wife.

In January 2022, my family contracted COVID-19. My daughter caught the virus first. I believe she brought it home with her from school because there was an outbreak in her classroom.

My daughter was sick for a few days and then recovered. Then, I got sick for a few days and recovered.

My wife, however, did not fare so well. Her bout with COVID was minor at best. She was only sick for a few days. Then, she got better for a couple of days, to the point where we thought everything was back to normal. The next day, she woke up with extreme dizziness.

She also had strange visual disturbances that she described as "like being on a boat." Her symptoms persisted no matter what she did. When she rested, she was dizzy; when she was active, she was dizzy. Nothing seemed to alleviate it.

Days went by, then weeks. Both of us were starting to get

concerned. A quick Google search of long COVID symptoms was enough to send both of us into despair. I watched YouTube videos and newspaper articles about long COVID patients. So many of the patients spotlighted in articles couldn't work, and required around-the-clock care. Their prognosis hasn't improved.

Before this happened, my wife was a very high-functioning person. She is very much like me, able to do many things at the same time. She was pursuing a Master's degree, and she had all the responsibilities of a wife, mother, and daughter. To say that this disrupted her life is an understatement.

My wife went to every doctor you can think of: primary care, internal medicine, cardiologist, neurologist, ENT, pulmonologist, physical therapist (two types), chiropractor, and psychiatrist, and that's just scratching the surface. She wanted answers on why she was feeling this way, but most of the doctors just shrugged off her symptoms as anxiety. They were unwilling and unable to help.

Yet, my wife didn't stop. She wouldn't take no for an answer.

A long COVID clinic confirmed our suspicions—she indeed had long COVID. Before this, when I thought of long COVID, I thought of persistent flu-like symptoms. However, it is not that.

My wife's COVID only lasted a few days. All traces of it are gone from her system. However, we learned that by sheer bad luck, the infection spread to her ear, destroying the nerves there and causing minor hearing loss and a condition called labyrinthitis. Labyrinthitis is the inflammation of the inner ear. It lasts for a few days or weeks, but the long-term effects are devastating; they include severe dizziness that doesn't go away matter what you do, anxiety attacks, heart palpitations, visual disturbances, hearing loss, and many other symptoms. The disease presents similar to chronic fatigue syndrome (CFS) and pain disorders such as fibromyalgia.

The most important thing with labyrinthitis is to catch it early. Unfortunately for my wife, because of doctor incompetence, we did not catch the labyrinthitis as early as we could have. The result was a complete upheaval in my family's life.

My wife would suffer panic attacks for no reason. It turns out that when the nerves in your inner ear are destroyed, the brain perceives dizziness as life-threatening. Its response is to panic. If you have ever witnessed a *true* anxiety attack or experienced one yourself, then you know just how devastating they are to both the person experiencing it and the people around them. My wife had several anxiety attacks every day. When she got them, she wasn't herself. It was as if she transformed into another person. The experience is very much like watching someone have a seizure. The attacks left her disoriented and with no energy. They were very scary and emotionally draining for me.

Eventually, YouTube videos led us in the direction of discovering labyrinthitis. My wife suspected that she had it, and she had to raise the topic with her doctors. Not once did any doctor say, "We think you have labyrinthitis or a vestibular issue." She had to bring it up. If that's not an indictment on the United States healthcare system, I don't know what is.

After weeks of advocating for a labyrinthitis diagnosis, my wife eventually found a doctor who requested that she do a VGN test.

In reading about VGN tests, I thought they were relatively benign, like a CT scan or an MRI. No—this test was hell. They attach many sensors to your head to track your nerve function. Then, they induce vertigo to see how your body reacts. My wife says that it was the most hellish experience she has ever endured in her life. It left her shaken, disoriented, and unable to function for a week.

Fortunately, the VGN test confirmed the labyrinthitis diagnosis. Finally having a diagnosis was a huge sigh of relief for us. After dozens of tests, we ruled out that she didn't have cancer, she wasn't going to have a heart attack, she didn't have a brain tumor, and that despite the gravity of the symptoms, she wasn't in any mortal danger. The doctors told her that it would take anywhere from 9 to 18 months for her to make a full recovery, and even then, the doctors weren't entirely sure about her prognosis because this bout of labyrinthitis was brought on by COVID-19. There's a lot that the medical community still doesn't know about COVID-19.

My wife's symptoms got so bad that she had to take short-term disability at work. The prospects of my wife not making a full recovery and never working again weighed heavily on me as it was possible that I would have to be the sole provider in my household. I'm fortunate enough to have a good job, but this sort of change in a household would be difficult for any family to absorb. To say I was worried about our finances and financial future is putting it lightly.

My wife and I both have made very smart financial decisions in life. We paid off our student debt early. In fact, we have no debt. We are very careful with our finances and we have been diligent about saving for retirement. The fact that we made all those smart decisions, did what we were supposed to do, and we *still* could have been wiped out by this incident is another indictment of the political and economic atmosphere here in the United States.

You would think that, in the middle of a pandemic, citizens would be able to get healthcare that is not tied to an employer. You would also think that, with incidents of long COVID being so common, it would be easier for people to get short-term disability, medical care, and benefits such as therapy and mental health counseling that they need in a time like this.

At the time of this writing, there are no benefits available to me and my wife as a result of this crisis. We had to navigate it alone. We have healthcare through my wife's job; if she loses her job or has to quit, we won't have healthcare and we'll have to buy gap insurance until I can enroll my family with my employer's health insurance plan. Private insurance is extremely expensive.

All those medical bills we have to pay for—that's our responsibility. Any permanent and long-lasting medical conditions that my wife will inevitably have as a result of this crisis are her responsibility.

What are world governments doing to address this problem? My wife was one of the lucky ones. There will be more people who, before catching COVID, were healthy, high-functioning, ambitious, industrious, and independent people. When they suddenly can no longer take care of themselves or find themselves facing bankruptcy or some other godforsaken reality, our governments will do nothing. If they do anything at all, it will be to punish those who were not lucky or rich enough to survive a personal health crisis.

As horrible as the pandemic has been so far with the lives we've lost, the worst is yet to come with long COVID.

One of my wife's long COVID doctors told her that COVID is really a mental disease. Its physical effects do not last very long. The mental effects are the most devastating. To paraphrase what he said, "We are finding that for many of our patients, COVID has rewired their brains to make them feel as if they are constantly under attack and still fighting the disease even though it has left their body. It is similar to post-traumatic stress disorder. Therefore, the recommendations we have been making to patients have been not only to treat the physical symptoms as they appear, but also to retrain their brains to function in this new neural condition that COVID has caused."

We already have a mental health crisis here in the United States with drugs, opioid addiction, mass shootings, and veteran suicides, to name just a few symptoms. If COVID is literally and figuratively putting people out of their minds, I can't imagine what this world will be like in another decade after COVID has had the opportunity to infect, reinfect, and devastate a significant amount of the world population with long COVID and its associated symptoms and conditions.

My wife and I have a long road ahead of us, but the day I wrote this chapter, we got promising test results that indicated that she is most definitely on the right path to recovery. Every day is a new struggle, but things are getting better.

This experience has completely changed my wife's life. She had to lean very hard into her faith. It has made her a stronger person, but she will not be the same person she was before January 14, 2022, when she got her positive COVID diagnosis.

I share all of this because the *Indie Author Confidential* series is my way of articulating lessons that I've learned on my path to becoming a successful author. Boy, did I learn many lessons from this experience.

I learned something that I always feared: life can strike at any time. I've been careful in my writing life to prepare for this as much as possible. This is why I created a course in 2020 called *Writing in Hard Times*. In that course, I outline my strategies for dealing with life's struggles as they arise. You can't prepare for everything, but you can damn well try. Looking back, that was a smart move, and it confirmed that I was definitely thinking about my career (and life) in the right manner.

I also learned the power of optimism. During a time like this, it is easy to fall into despair. During the first few months of this crisis, I had no idea what was going to happen to my wife.

Yet, I stayed optimistic. Even when it was hard, I found a silver lining in every day, in every diagnosis, and in every interaction with a doctor. I don't know if it ultimately made a difference, but I know that it helped *me* keep a clear perspective. That helped me support her.

I learned the power of momentum. I stepped away from my writing for a few weeks to help my wife through this difficult time. Not once did I have any regrets. Not once did I wallow over the fact that I couldn't get any words. I dealt with the problem, set a date to return, and I returned.

I kept working even when it was easier not to do so. Even though I took time off from writing, I still continued making progress in my writing business every day. I published several books. I traveled to writing conferences and appeared as a guest on podcasts. I kept making YouTube videos. I produced two audiobooks, fixed typos in my books, and did other things that I had a better mental capacity for. As a result, most people didn't even know I was away. I continued writing my nightly blog, even though I had nothing to say on many of those days.

Everything in life is a season. Just as summer cannot be endless, neither can a personal crisis. I knew that my future self would appreciate it if I kept even just a modicum of momentum during this crisis. That's what I did. This year, I am still on track to have one of my best word count years ever.

I also learned the true sweetness of that age-old quote, "Be kind to everyone you meet for they are fighting a great battle." I always liked that quote; I like it a lot more now.

This chapter is just to show you that everyone in life goes through hard times. You may be going through a hard time in your life right now. It won't last forever.

I'm sure that, in the grand scheme of the universe, there was some reason that my wife and I were chosen to go through this.

We may never know, but at least we made it. What got us through was faith, optimism, and prior preparation.

If you are not going through a hard time right now, one is sure to come. That's why I recommend taking steps now to prepare and plan. For writers, this means learning new ways to write, thinking about the future, and streamlining your existing production processes. I have detailed much of my experience in these areas in the *Indie Author Confidential* series.

AUTOMATED WEBSITES

I stumbled across a service that offers website creation for authors. That in and of itself is not unique, but the way this company approached creating those websites was.

I have said several times throughout this series that maintaining an author website becomes more challenging as you become prolific. It's a relatively easy affair to update your site when you only have one or two books. When you have 80 books, and you realize that you need to update something, you have to do it 80 times...

For example, I recently had a bug in my website that was causing some of the links on my book pages to be invalid, but I didn't know which pages were affected. I had to go through every book page and test every link. That was a pain.

Other little problems come up from time to time that add up in the long run. That's why I have said that the next website I build will utilize automation for gathering the metadata for my books. I don't know what that automation will look like, but this website service that I am going to discuss offers an intriguing solution.

The idea is this: instead of building a website page for each of your books, the service gives you templates to choose from and then scrapes the data off your Amazon sales page. Any time you update the sales page, your website will also be updated overnight. The service also crawls retailer websites regularly, so when you publish a new book, it will automatically create a page on your site.

This is ingenious. I thought the best way to handle this would be through building a database using my master publishing file as the basis, but this is much more economical if you think about it. Your sales pages are always up-to-date. If such a service were to take off, it would virtually eliminate the issue of website maintenance for your book pages. You would only have to monitor your pages from time to time (which you could do adequately with WordPress plug-ins). Under this model, an author who has hundreds of books would spend almost as much time maintaining their site as an author with only one or two books. Of course, there will always be issues endemic to large portfolios, but this is the type of solution we should be encouraging in the community.

There were a few things I didn't like about the service in question—namely that it is still early and the functionality is limited. The service also didn't take into consideration authors like me; it is mostly targeting new authors at this time. That's why I am not mentioning the name. However, I believe their business model is a sound one, and if they offer customizable and dynamic templates, infinite scaling, and relatively few bugs, I believe this is the future of author websites.

I'm so glad I found a service like this because it challenged me to think about the future of my own author website.

THE RISE OF CANCEL CULTURE

At a conference, a best-selling author used a certain outdated term to refer to black people. The author was praising another member of the panel who was black.

The author who made the remarks could be considered elderly and is a product of a different era.

I'm not going to mention names in this post because the names aren't important.

Many in the community quickly labeled this person as a racist and demanded a boycott of their books. The controversy spread like wildfire. As usual, people split into two camps: those who were against this author because this person was a purported racist, and those who supported this author (who were labeled by the other side as purported racists too). A prominent author organization disavowed the author, despite having given this person its most prestigious award the year before. The award was revoked.

As a black person, I understand the concern around the use of the term in question and why some people were offended by it. I wouldn't have been, though I would have certainly tilted my head at this author if she referred to me using the term. I would have pulled her aside afterward and said something to her. I have seen nothing online previously to suggest that this author hates black people.

I don't believe that the majority of people in this country are racist. Ignorance is a far more widespread problem, but ignorance is not the same as racism. Trust me, I would know.

I grew up in St. Louis, Missouri, which is one of the most segregated cities in the United States, even today. My great-grandparents were sharecroppers and picked cotton in the Deep South. They told me stories of what real racism was like. My great-grandfather fled Mississippi because if he hadn't, he would have been on the shortlist to be lynched.

My grandparents grew up before the civil rights movement, and they fought a type of racism that doesn't exist today, particularly in the workplace.

During my elementary years, I was the victim of overt racism at least twice (that I know of). These experiences weren't someone making an offhand remark about me; they were life-altering.

I went to college in a small town in Iowa, where many people never had an interaction with a black person. There were definitely ignorant people, but I wouldn't call (most) of the people I went to school with racist. I say that because my freshman year, I lived a few doors down from a self-described white supremacist. He broadcasted it publicly and he was proud of it. I had several conversations with him. I learned a lot from those encounters. Because of that, I know racists when I see them. Most people are not racists.

My point is that many of these people pointing fingers and crying "racist" have probably never met a real one. If they did, they would choose their words more carefully.

You can't talk to a racist. They can't be reasoned with. You *can*, however, have a reasonable conversation with an ignorant person and change their perspective. When two rational people have a conversation, both walk away having learned something. That's the point of discourse. It makes us better.

All these allegations of racism against people who may or may not be racist is ultimately hurting everyone. Calling someone a racist is an easy way to shut that person down. When people hear the term, they lose the ability to think critically. If someone is racist, how could you support them? No one wants to be affiliated with one, and rightfully so.

I have no love for racists, but I object to people using allegations of racism to advance a political ideology or personal agenda. To call someone a racist should be, as it has always been, a very grave allegation reserved for the worst that society has to offer—not cheaply thrown around on social media as a way to make a statement to people you don't know (and who don't care about you) on what your values are.

It appears that this author is going to suffer considerably from this fallout, and I don't believe it was justified. No one in the community should be able to make unfounded allegations and destroy someone's career so easily.

I think about authors who have been canceled due to their words or actions. Maybe the backlash against some was justified, but if even one innocent person loses their livelihood because of something that could have been a teachable moment, that is a human tragedy. That doesn't give people license to keep saying bad things, but we have to have some compassion and grace and pray that people can learn from their mistakes. We should extend the same compassion and grace that we would want extended to us.

Everyone should be allowed to publish the books they want on their own terms. Every reader has a right to purchase the books that they are interested in. If you don't like someone's politics or someone's views on a certain matter, then don't buy that book and don't support that author. If you don't like the politics of a conference or a publishing house, then don't support that conference or publishing house.

People seem to forget that the writing profession is a business of opinions. Everybody has opinions. Some of those opinions will probably offend you. *Your* opinions will probably offend somebody else.

Whether it's a remark at a conference or written opinions in a book, having to deal with things we disagree with (sometimes viscerally) is the cost of living in a free society. When someone says something ignorant, they *should* be corrected. But when we start trying to censor others, we start down a slippery slope that, at some point, will be so slippery that we can't turn back.

When all we focus on is identity politics, we risk losing our own identities as authors.

R.A.M.P-ING UP MY CAREER

I have been focused on improving my discipline as a writer. I'm already pretty disciplined, but I believe I can improve.

One area I am trying to improve is balancing my daily activities. I love to write, so that's where I spend the majority of my time. I'm happiest when I am in the land of a new story.

However, I am so focused on word production that sometimes other areas of my business drop off for a time. This results in an ever-growing mountain of emails, tax receipts that need to be organized, and other obligations that I need to attend to that I put off for a few days when I am in the heat of finishing a book.

I need to take a more balanced approach to my writing life.

My strategy as a writer is as follows:

1. Become a world-class content creator
2. Become a technology and data-driven writer
3. Become the writer of the future.

What are the tactics that I need to be taking every single day to support that strategy?

I came up with an acronym that explains the four key activities I should be doing every day. The acronym is R.A.M.P.

R is for reading.

A is for analyzing data and opportunities.

M is for marketing.

P is for production of books, specifically, new words every day.

The question I have been asking myself every day for the last few months has been, "What does the picture of good look like today?" That is a great question because it keeps me focused on what I am doing every day to further my career. However, the question often leads me down rabbit holes.

I have changed the question. Instead, I ask, "What am I doing to R.A.M.P. up my career today?"

In other words:

- What did I read today?
- How did I use data in some capacity to glean an insight into the business?
- How did I market today?
- How many words did I write?

I have a daily blog where I talk about my activities for the day. I have built a great community of people who have been interested in my day-to-day adventures. I adopted the R.A.M.P. acronym as a way to structure the blog posts so that they're easy to scan.

My R.A.M.P. posts hit the highlights of everything I did that day. They have been a hit with my community.

Each letter of the acronym allows for a jumping-off point for my posts:

- I might be reading a book where the author used a technique that captivated me. I will talk about that technique generally on the blog (and in this series).
- If I uncover an interesting insight with my advertising, sales, or dictation, I discuss those on the blog too.
- I talk about things I'm doing to market my work.
- And--most popularly--I share my word count for the day and how my writing sessions went.

Developing the R.A.M.P. acronym and sticking to it has been helpful for me in keeping my priorities straight.

ENCOUNTER WITH A SAVVY
AUTHOR ESTATE

This quarter, I had a run-in with a savvy author estate. Given that I wrote two books on estate planning this year, I have been paying careful attention to author estates.

I happened to be on a speaking panel on Zoom, and afterward, one of the audience members reached out to thank me for the advice I gave on the panel. This person was the personal representative for a very wealthy author estate that you would recognize. After a nice email exchange, the representative asked for my address to send me a care package. I was blown away by what I received, not only because it was very generous, but because it was a master class in author branding and marketing.

Here is what it contained:

- several handsome paperback copies of the author's books
- bookmarks
- audiobooks of the works on a USB drive that was branded to the cover of one of the author's books
- a brochure with more of the author's works and appropriate links

- a handwritten note

Wow. It was impressive. It set the kind of standard that I want to achieve myself one day. It would be easy to send a reader a paperback copy of my work, a bookmark, a copy of the audiobook, and a brochure, along with a handwritten note. That is stunningly easy. It's so easy that I kicked myself that I had never thought of it.

My encounter with this estate is proof that it is indeed possible to make long-term plans for your work and have people continue your legacy long after you're gone. It inspired me to double down on my estate planning efforts. If I'm lucky, I will leave an estate that can operate on such a high professional level.

THIS TIME LAST YEAR

I thought it would be fun to continue a segment every Q3 that looks back at previous volumes to see how I have advanced and how the industry has changed.

What was happening a year ago in Q3 2021? Some of the things that were important for me:

- Things were starting to return to normal after a crazy 2020. My family began going out to restaurants for the first time since 2020.
- It was a little easier to plan for the future. The hysteria of the pandemic was starting to wear off.
- Honestly, as I think back to Q3 2021, it was...kind of boring. Looking back on it, that's a wonderful thing.

Content Creation

. . .

This time last year, I wrapped up many responsibilities that were draining me every day: law school, podcasting, and teaching insurance classes. I didn't realize the gains at the time, but ceasing these activities allowed me to be more disciplined.

Technology and Data

This time last year, I was experimenting with AI tools. Most were dead-ends.

Become the Writer of the Future

Ironically, I commented on Google Play's auto-narration tool. I said this: "That said, I downloaded a few public domain titles and listened to them. The narration wasn't good, but it wasn't bad either. It clearly sounded like an AI was reading the book, but it sounded a hell of a lot better than current voice-to-text software on phones and computers. The voice still reads too fast and doesn't handle sentence breaks or proper nouns well. Still, it's promising.

"With any new technology, people are quick to judge or write it off without understanding the rate at which technology advances. I'd give Google's effort a C-. In five years, however, if they continue the program and continue improving the technology, it'll be a B+ or an A-, enough for customers to start paying attention. Then, overnight, the technology will be mainstream and everyone will be using it."

Wow.

A few chapters later, I wrote about how authors are tired of

AI. They just don't seem to be interested in the new tools that are popping up. I wrote, "I suggest that it is up to you to figure out your artificial intelligence strategy. At this point, no one is going to do it for you, and I don't see anyone dedicating themselves to creating advanced tools to help authors as a whole. If they do, they'll do it without too much input from the authors who need it most—those who will be left behind."

Now, here we are in 2022. What a year.

THIS TIME FIVE YEARS AGO

I was thinking about how far I've come compared to five years ago. I'll continue my trip into (not so) old memories.

In 2017, I wrote a 9-book space opera series called *Galaxy Mavericks*. In July 2017, I was just wrapping up the publication of the series. I had a blast writing it. I wrote the entire series before launching it. Almost all of the major lessons I learned in 2017 came from *Galaxy Mavericks*.

Galaxy Mavericks was the series that taught me the importance of branded covers. In 2016, I started a campaign to clean up my covers and make them more consistent. I followed a similar style for all my books moving forward, with my author name prominently at the top of my covers. When you have 9 books that have a consistent look, it looks GREAT on a bookshelf. With this series as the visual anchor, all the books in my portfolio started to gel visually.

Galaxy Mavericks also taught me the importance of research, and that I wasn't doing my research correctly. I got the space details in that story horribly wrong, but readers still loved the story. I would carry the research mistakes I made from this book to my future series.

Galaxy Mavericks also contains the fastest novel I've ever written to date. *Zero Magnitude* (Book 3) clocked in at six days. I still haven't written a faster novel since.

Galaxy Mavericks also taught me how to write books out of sequence. I wrote Book 2 first, then 1,3,4,5,6,7,8, and 9. It also taught me a tremendous amount about writing into the dark. To write a 9-book series without an outline is a gigantic feat.

2017 was a good year, but for some reason, it's not as prominent in my memory as 2018. We'll talk about that next year!

THIS TIME TEN YEARS AGO

Since we're on the topic of traveling back in time, I might as well look at the last decade…

July 2022 is exactly 10 years to the month that I had my near-death experience. This time 10 years ago, I was leaving the hospital.

In July 2012, I fell ill with food poisoning after eating a nice dinner at a restaurant. My wife rushed me to the hospital… where I didn't leave for a month. I had food poisoning but then picked up an infection in the hospital, and doctors almost didn't catch it. The only reason I survived was because of sheer luck. My wife's old roommate was in medical school at the time, and when she heard about my symptoms, she told me what to tell the doctors…and then they discovered what was really wrong.

In fact, an article came out in the *USA Today* newspaper about the type of infection I caught and how it was killing people across the country, mainly because of bureaucracy, lack of sanitation, and inaction on the part of hospitals. The article is titled "Far More Could Be Done to Stop the Deadly C. Diff Bacteria."

It is dated August 16, 2012, which is right around the time I got out of the hospital. It honestly might have been that exact week; I can't remember. I used to have a paper copy of the newspaper, but it's probably long gone now. I kept it to remind me of what my life was like at the lowest point.

While I was in the hospital, I asked myself what I was doing with my life. I worked a crappy job as a claims adjuster (and got yelled at every day, all day, in English and Spanish), I had a ridiculous amount of student loan debt (loans were half my paycheck), a car payment that took up another third of my check, I lived in a tiny studio apartment, and I had only written some short stories and poems that no one would look at. I had some novel ideas, but agents wouldn't even give me the time of day.

I swore on that hospital bed that I would become a writer and I didn't care what I had to do to make it happen.

This time, ten years ago, I got out of the hospital, recovered fully, and shortly afterward, I discovered self-publishing. I'm pretty sure it was "The Creative Penn" first, followed shortly by The Alliance of Independent Authors (which was founded in 2012). I learned what was possible, and I couldn't wait to try it for myself. A few months later, I came up with the concept for my first novel: *How to Be Bad* (now *Magic Souls*), and I spent the entirety of 2013 learning about self-publishing, learning how to write my first book, and working with my first editor (Gary Smailes at BubbleCow, an amazing guy). I spent $40 on a pre-made cover from Goonwrite.com. I bought Scrivener for $35.

On January 6, 2014, *How to Be Bad/Magic Souls* was finally published. Three people bought it: me (because I wanted to generate a sales rank for the book), my writing buddy at the time, and my mom. I made $5.79 in January 2014 and somewhere around $50 total for the book during that first year.

Yikes. I made just about every tactical error you can think

of, but I kept listening to podcasts, reading blogs and books, buying paid courses (if I could afford them), and asked people in the community for advice. Somehow, I survived that first year without doing anything too stupid.

Fast-forward a decade later and it's crazy how far I've come. Joanna Penn was the person who got me into self-publishing; this year, I'll be on her show for the third time. ALLi gave me a lot of confidence and helped me find good information; I'm the Outreach Manager at ALLi now and have done countless podcasts & speaking events on their behalf. I even wrote a book for them.

I work a much better job now (thank god), I have written more books than I ever dreamed of, I'm constantly amazed by my book sales, and I'm especially amazed by how many people recognize me at speaking events. I've been published in "Writer's Digest," spoken at countless events, and have a pretty recognizable name in the indie space. Sure, I'm not a full-time author yet, but I definitely am on a path to getting there.

All of this took ten years. Ten years. Put another way, I'll be 35 this year. This took nearly a third of my life. And I've still got a long way to go.

If you're wondering whether the writing life is for you, keep at it. Keep writing. Keep reading. Keep learning. With every book you publish, aim to make at least one fewer mistake. Stay optimistic no matter how crappy things get. Get a mentor. Keep learning business, copyright, covers, book descriptions, etc. Dreams do come true!

Q3 2022 PROGRESS REPORT

I'm now two-thirds of the way through 2022. It has been a good year so far. Here is the progress I've made toward my goals.

BECOME A WORLD-CLASS CONTENT CREATOR

To achieve my goal of becoming a world-class content creator, I will focus on the following tactical priorities:

- Demonstrate a commitment to learning the craft of storytelling and teaching
- Demonstrate a commitment to outstanding quality AND quantity

Examples of day-to-day activities that will help me carry out my tactical priorities include:

- Keep learning through online courses and workshops taught by professional writers who are further down the path I want to write
- Reading
- Developing mentorships
- Finding new ways to increase my daily word counts
- Mastering different writing methods
- Documenting my process of becoming a successful writer in the *Indie Author Confidential* series
- Cleaning up my platform to ensure a consistent quality reader experience

What did I do to become a world-class content creator during Q3 2022?

1. I secured a mentor who is a very successful indie author.
2. I have read (and studied the craft in) 30 books so far this year.
3. I am still on track to publish 100 books by end of 2023.
4. I exploded my dictation word counts with a voice recorder and Microsoft Word macros.

BECOME A TECHNOLOGY AND DATA-DRIVEN WRITER

To achieve my goal of becoming a technology and data-driven writer, I will focus on the following tactical priorities:

- Use technology to make the business more efficient
- Use data to get insights

Examples of day-to-day activities that will help me carry out my tactical priorities include:

- Developing a tax plan
- Developing an estate plan assisted with technology
- Learning how to design my own covers
- Hiring a personal assistant for small tasks where it makes sense
- Developing a metadata database for my work
- Improving my readers' experience on my website
- Implementing direct sales for my fiction

What did I do to become a more technology and data-driven writer during Q2 2022?

1. I learned how to run profitable Facebook Ads and had one of my best sales months ever.
2. I developed a killer Microsoft Word macro for cleaner and faster dictation and transcription.

As with this quarter, I will continue doing more of the same: focusing on growing my portfolio to 100 titles and focusing on maximizing the value of my portfolio through new formats and quality assessments. I will also ramp up my lessons in cover design in the final quarter of the year.

As I said at the end of 2021, 2022 is the final year for me to get my fundamentals right. I'm excited about that, and I'm looking forward to what the end of the year brings.

CONTENT CREATED WHILE WRITING THIS BOOK

This section recaps the books I've published and media I've created during the quarter. To keep the book evergreen, I will not include links to podcasts or magazine articles because sometimes links break over time, especially with podcasts if the hosts stop podcasting. You can easily search for them to see if they're still active at the time you're reading this book. If they are, enjoy! If not, please accept my apologies.

Books

Year of the Rat (*The Chicago Rat Shifter*, Book 3). The third and final novel in Michael's wildest urban fantasy yet. Cyrus Grant searches for a way to cure his sister from the grips of a demon possession. The cure? A ruthless demon collector who peddles in lies and shadows.

Buy at: https://www.michaellaronn.com/yearoftherat

Grab the complete trilogy at: https://www.michaellaronn.com/ratshiftertrilogy/ratshiftertrilogy

Learn more about *The Chicago Rat Shifter* series: https://www.michaellaronn.com/ratshifter

Podcast/Video Appearances

"Estate Planning for Authors" on The Creative Penn
Michael and Joanna Penn talk about all things estate planning for authors, and how you can organize your affairs and leave a legacy for your family.

"How Get the Most Out of In-Person Speaking Events" on The Indy Author Podcast
Michael and Matty Dalrymple talk about their experience at the 2022 Writer's Digest Annual Conference, along with tips about how to maximize your experience at in-person speaking events.

READ THE NEXT VOLUME

Michael's writer journey continues in the next volume of this series!

Grab your copy at www.authorlevelup.com/confidential.

MEET M.L. RONN

Science fiction and fantasy on the wild side!

M.L. Ronn (Michael La Ronn) is the author of many science fiction and fantasy novels including *The Good Necromancer*, *Android X,* and *The Last Dragon Lord* series.

In 2012, a life-threatening illness made him realize that storytelling was his #1 passion. He's devoted his life to writing ever since, making up whatever story makes him fall out of his chair laughing the hardest. Every day.

Learn more about Michael
www.authorlevelup.com (for writers)
www.michaellaronn.com (fiction)

MORE BOOKS BY M.L. RONN

Books for Writers:

www.authorlevelup.com/books

Fiction:
www.michaellaronn.com/books